A *For Better or For Worse*® Special Edition

All About

Our little girl grows up!

by Lynn Johnston

Andrews McMeel
Publishing

Kansas City

www.FBorFW.com

01 02 03 04 05 BAH 10 9 8 7 6 5 4 3 2

ISBN: 0-7407-2063-5

Library of Congress Catalog Card Number: 2001095920

For Charles (Sparky) Schulz
Who never stopped being a kid.

Other For Better or For Worse® Collections

Graduation: A Time for Change
The Big 5-0
Sunshine and Shadow
Middle Age Spread
Growing Like a Weed
Love Just Screws Everything Up
Starting from Scratch
"There Goes My Baby!"
Things Are Looking Up . . .
What, Me Pregnant?
If This Is a Lecture, How Long Will It Be?
Pushing 40
It's All Downhill from Here
Keep the Home Fries Burning
The Last Straw
Just One More Hug
"It Must Be Nice to Be Little"
Is This "One of Those Days," Daddy?
I've Got the One-More-Washload Blues . . .

Retrospectives

The Lives Behind the Lines: 20 Years of For Better or For Worse®
Remembering Farley: A Tribute to the Life of Our Favorite Cartoon Dog
It's the Thought That Counts . . . Fifteenth Anniversary Collection
A Look Inside . . . For Better or For Worse: The 10th Anniversary Collection

Little Books

Isn't He Beautiful?
Isn't She Beautiful?
Wags and Kisses
A Perfect Christmas

Call it a surprise, call it a gift, call it a challenge—Elly Patterson was pregnant again and completely unprepared for more responsibility.

After the discovery, she confided first in her friend Connie and then in her husband, John. Sitting on the edge of the bed they shared, he put his arm around her and she cried.

In her mind, life was beginning to get easier. Their two older children, Michael and Elizabeth, were independent, capable of going out on their own. They understood the words "no," "or else," and "over my dead body!!!" And even though they rarely did so, they knew how to clean up after themselves.

It was already a perfect family, in a house with the right number of rooms. "I don't want to turn into a blimp again!" she sniveled. "I want to go back to school, have a career—be something!"

Being a parent is something.

When baby began to move, Elly began to accept her. When her tummy swelled with kicking, pushing life, she caressed it with her hands and wondered, "Who are you?" As the arrival time drew near, she was ready and she hoped that the others would be ready too.

Baby arrived without warning. She was consistent! On a stormy night with two neighbors to help her, Elly delivered a beautiful dark-haired baby girl.

John, who had been delayed by the weather, came home to find his wife and children holding the baby they had named for the month she was born. April Patterson came into the world on the first of April 1991—changing the Patterson family forever—and for the better.

DAD! DAD! IT'S A GIRL! MOM HAD A BABY GIRL!

WHY DID YOU CALL HER APRIL?

BECAUSE IT'S A LOVELY NAME AND A LOVELY MONTH.

APRIL IS WARM DAYS, FRESH FLOWERS, NESTING BIRDS....

YEAH....

AN' IT ALSO RAINS A LOT.

LOOK, LIZ. IF YOU STROKE APRIL'S CHEEK, SHE TURNS HER HEAD TOWARD YOUR TOUCH.

WHY?

IT'S CALLED A "ROOTING REFLEX". IT'S AN AUTOMATIC SEARCHING RESPONSE FOR FOOD.

WHEN DOES IT STOP?

CLANK ROOT MUNCH SEARCH

... IT DOESN'T.

Elly's breasts swelled again with milk, counters became repositories for change pads, soothers, creams, and wet-wipes.

For Michael and Elizabeth, the novelty of having a beautiful new sister quickly evaporated as the reality of responsibility sunk in.

The sports car John had circled in *Auto Buff Monthly* was forgotten as a car seat, folding stroller, and travel bed were purchased to facilitate the comfort and safe transportation of baby.

Everything was new. Crib, toys, clothes—everything. Elly had generously given up their baby paraphernalia to friends, family, and the local thrift shop. After all, she had two school-aged kids and a dog. There'd be no need for a diaper pail now!

For a while, April "slept" in a borrowed basket in Elly and John's bedroom. Although they'd twice adjusted themselves to the shock of 3 A.M. feedings, their ability to cope with sleep deprivation once more had diminished markedly. It's hard to sing lullabies while you're yawning.

When feedings became fewer and sleep more assured, April was moved into Elizabeth's room. There was just enough space if you pushed her bed against the wall to fit a crib and a change table. Elizabeth now shared what had been her own private space, a little begrudgingly, a little with pride.

It was tough for the older kids to see so much attention being lavished on someone whose only signs of gratitude were grunts and gas-grins. Still, they were loving and attentive and learned to handle the newcomer.

Babies cling to you. Clasping your hips with their legs, they ride as if on a trusted steed carrying them from one adventure to another. Mike and Liz became accustomed to the lively new appendage. It was cool to watch the new kid grow and learn things . . . to experiment with stuff like "how many times can I spit out this banana before I actually have to swallow it?"

MOMMY AND DADDY ARE GOING OUT FOR SUPPER, APRIL! BABY'S GOING TO BE A GOOD GIRL AND STAY HOME!

SHE'S GOING TO PLAY, AND SHE'S GOING TO HAVE A BATH AND SHE'S GOING TO HAVE SUCH A GOOOD TIME!

APRIL'S GOING TO STAY WITH BIG BROTHER! ISN'T THAT NICE? SHE'S A LUCKY BABY!—YES SHE IS !!

WAAAAHHHHH

GASP!—IT'S AMAZING WHAT YOU CAN GET DONE IN 10 MINUTES!

GRAK GRAK CLANK

SWING-A-TOT

CLANK GRAK GRAK

....THAT'S HOW LONG THE WIND-UP SWING LASTS.

CLIK CLAK CLIK CLAK

Jolly jumpers, wind-up swings, learning and activity toys were all designed to promote one thing—good mental and physical health. Yours.

Anything that provides five minutes or more "diversion" time is worth its weight in wet-wipes. Likewise, a good baby-sitter is part of the survival kit. Elly used all these devices with a clear conscience . . . and April continued to grow.

Someone wise once said, "If you're going to toss a baby into the air . . . make sure she hasn't just eaten."

Friends whose kids were grown soon remembered what it was like to have a baby of their own again.

With April in their arms, they remembered the funny faces, the round little body, the movements, and the mannerisms.

They remembered the hugs and the hazards, the laughter and the tears, the odors of powder and poo.

They remembered peek-a-boo and bouncing baby on their knees.

They remembered all these things and their hearts swelled with sentiment and joy . . . as they handed April back to Elly and went home.

Even when it's kid number three, few events are more exciting than Baby's first Christmas. With red velvet outfits and too many toys, April celebrated the birth of Jesus, as he would have done . . . and slept through it all.

MOM! LOOKIT HOW FAST APRIL CAN CRAWL NOW!

BET YOU CAN HARDLY WAIT 'TIL SHE'S WALKING!

Once April was mobile, nothing was safe. If it was unlocked, she'd open it, if it was on the floor, she'd eat it. Outlets were covered, cabinets were locked, and the dog sensitized himself to the slap-slap-slap of tiny hands on the hallway floor—for this meant possible pain.

SHE'S GROWING UP, MOM, SHE'S ALMOST WALKING. SHE'S MAKING MORE SOUNDS AND REALLY WANTS TO TALK! SAY HI TO GRANDMA!

SHE TALKS ALL THE TIME NOW! -IT'S HARD TO KEEP HER QUIET! -JUST LISTEN!

WELL, I GUESS SHE'S NOT IN THE MOOD. -I'LL CALL AGAIN SOON. TAKE CARE! UH HUH...'BYE!

DA DADA DAH!! GA-GAH-GBLT! DOOOO DOOOO DEEE DEEE DEEDEE AGGLAG GLAGGLAG ABBABA DADADADAD OOHHGGL

By her first birthday, April was taking her first steps. More things in the busy world around her were coming within reach. The cooing sounds of "you can do it" soon changed to "ah ah ah" and "NO!!" Why is it that all the most interesting stuff is forbidden?

I CAN'T BELIEVE APRIL'S A YEAR OLD ALREADY! THINGS SEEM TO HAPPEN IN THE BLINK OF AN EYE!

SHE'S INTO 18-MONTH OUTFITS, SHE'S INTO TODDLER TOYS, SHE'S INTO A FULL-SIZED CRIB...

SHE'S INTO THE FLOUR BIN!!!

WHAT HAPPENED?

...I BLINKED.

SPLRP!

SLAM BAM!

SQUISH!

GABRLTT

THOK!

THUNK BAM THUNK BAM THUNK BAM THUNK BAM THUNK BAM THUNK BAM THUNK BAM THUNK BAM THUNK BAM

EEEEEE AAAAAAA EEEAAAAA AAHHHHH

AT LAST!!

SNRK SNFF SNOZZZ

AHHH...THERE'S NOTHING QUITE AS BEAUTIFUL AS A SLEEPING BABY!

ALL THE FRUSTRATION, ALL THE TROUBLES THEY CAUSE, ALL THE SLEEPLESS NIGHTS SEEM TO MELT AWAY AS YOU GAZE AT THAT DEAR, SLEEPING LITTLE FACE.

....LUCKY FOR THEM!

Elly went back to work at the library, leaving her toddler in the care of her next-door-neighbor, Annie.

She felt guilty about going away every morning, but Annie's desire to add a daughter to her family of two sons made her an eager surrogate mom.

With sons Chris and Richard in school, April was the center of attention. Many things she was not allowed to do at home, she could pull off at Annie's. Annie never went anywhere without April on her hip. Like Mom, she played and read stories to her. She made Jell-O stars and sugar cookies. She created faces out of meatloaf, peas, and bagel bits and when it was time for April to return home at the end of the day, it was hard to let her go.

April now had two mothers, two families, and two sets of rules to follow. At Annie's she could eat in front of the TV, but not at home. At home she had to share and put things back where they belonged—but at Annie's her every wish came true. Tough scene!

For a while, Elly wondered why simple routines were met with hysterics. There were tantrums on the toilet and crying in the crib. The cherub she had left with Annie in the morning was a monster at night.

It took awhile before the two mothers came to an understanding. Some rules were consistently enforced, others could be relaxed.

April soon preferred the house with the rules . . . even though Annie's way seemed easier.

April's first word was "Gah!" There was some discussion as to whether she meant "Dad" or "doggie," but it got a good reaction. Her second word was "No" and the third was "Mama." After that, everyone lost count.

*O*ften, dads don't really connect to their kids until they start talking. John had always done the stuff that dads were expected to do, but it wasn't until April could actually communicate that the two bonded like glue.

Actually, one of their first intimate father-daughter moments was when April glued her hands together while John was making a plastic model in his workshop. He soaked her hands in solvent; he washed and carefully separated them—thankful that something awful and serious hadn't happened . . . like his wife finding out.

April loved the workshop. She played in the sawdust and she poked at the paints. It wasn't long before John was showing her how to use a hammer.

His third child, he knew, would be mechanical! April wanted to know how things worked and what they were made of. She learned what tools were for. She learned that taking stuff apart was much easier than putting it back together and she learned to admire the man who seemed to be able to do or make or fix anything.

For Better or For Worse
By Lynn Johnston

MINE!!

MINE!

MINE!

MINE, MINE, MINE, MINE, MINE, MINE MINE.

MINE!!

*B*irthdays and Christmas always seem to mark the milestones in our lives. For the Pattersons, these special days were best when grandparents came to stay.

Grandma Marian and Grandpa Jim often traveled all the way from British Columbia to see their daughter, Elly. Secretly, they wished she didn't live in Ontario. They'd always hoped she'd move with her family back to the west coast.

Still they enjoyed the trip and now they had a new granddaughter who changed so much between visits, she was like a brand-new child every time they saw her.

Grandma Marian did wonderful things, like bake bread and real ginger snaps. She knitted sweaters and taught big sister Elizabeth how to sew. She taught Michael how to type faster and how to write a letter—a good one— to a girl.

Grandpa was a storyteller, a man who could have been on the stage! With accents and gestures he'd describe a scene you could see in your mind so clearly; he could become one character and then another just by

SHE'S A BEAUTIFUL BABY, DEAR-AND, BUSY! VERY BUSY!

SHE'S JUST STARTED WALKING, DAD.-SHE'S INTO EVERYTHING!

I THINK WE SHOULD PUT SOME OF THE BREAKABLE THINGS OUT OF REACH.

YES!

...AND WE'LL BEGIN WITH ME.

shifting his position or changing the expression on his face. Grandpa Jim could make any book come alive!

So much good food came from the kitchen when the grandparents came to visit that even the dog gained weight! And when it was time to go, April wanted them to bundle her up in a suitcase and take her with them.

Goodbye was one of the hardest words she'd ever learned to say.

G'AMMA GO HOME, NOW?

YES, DEAR. IT'S BEEN A LOVELY HOLIDAY— BUT IT'S TIME TO GO.

PHIL'S HERE TO TAKE YOU TO THE AIRPORT, DAD. DO YOU HAVE YOUR BAGS?-YOUR TICKETS?

WE'RE ALL ORGANIZED, KIDS.

EVERYTHING WE'RE TAKING WITH US IS SITTING IN THE HALL!

If Elly and John ever argued, it was usually about discipline. Were they too easy? Were they too strict?

All three kids enjoyed the fact that they'd arrived on the planet without instruction manuals and that family rules were determined by two people who often questioned their own decisions.

For April, the youngest . . . life was good.

Survival of our species is dependent upon our ability to adapt. When circumstances change, you alter your way of life and carry on. But, kids thrive on routine. How do you painlessly guide your three-year-old from home care to day care? The answer is . . . you can't.

Elly smiled at the teacher, gave April an extra hug, and said goodbye. April looked around the room and decided to sit right where she was and cry until Mom came back to get her.

She didn't care if the chairs were just her size, she didn't care if the kids looked friendly. She didn't care about anything but going home.

After awhile, April agreed to try one glass of juice, and maybe a sandwich. A chocolate cake appeared and after the cake was gone, someone wiped her fingers with a warm, damp cloth. April realized she had unwittingly joined the ranks and perhaps day care wasn't all that bad after all.

This proves once more that kids and animals have much in common: both can be tamed with food.

For Better or For Worse

By Lynn Johnston

SHRIEK!

SEE, APRIL? THE SQUIRRELS ARE FILLING THEIR NESTS WITH FOOD—'CAUSE WINTER'S COMING!

THEY COLLECT SEEDS AN' NUTS AN' ALL KINDS OF GOOD STUFF!

THEN THEY HIDE IT AWAY IN A SAFE, WARM SECRET PLACE!

...SO THEY'LL HAVE SOMETHING TO EAT WHEN THE SNOW COMES!

A kid's first real Halloween is when they finally have it all figured out. They can't wait to put on their costumes, they can't wait to run from door to door where just a knock or the ring of the bell brings candies and treats of all kinds! So many houses, so little time.

After awhile, they tire out and fall asleep on Daddy's shoulder as he carries them home to bed. Later, both parents dutifully check out the loot to make sure everything's safe.

The next morning, what's left of the goodies is given back to the trick-or-treaters who probably won't notice that most of the best stuff is gone. As I said, a kid's first real Halloween is when they finally have it all figured out!

April loved her bed. She loved the feel and the sight and the sound of it. She loved her teddy and the glow of her night-light and the pink pajamas Grandma Carrie had made for her. She loved the softness of her pillow and the smoothness of the sheets.

April loved her bed. She just didn't like to be told when to go there.

All kids go through an assortment of flus and fevers, but each time an illness comes along, parent can't help worrying.

When April was sick, out came the supplies: water bottle, thermometer, cough syrup, and ear drops—whatever it took to make her feel better.

In the end, the best medicine was to hold her close and rock her to sleep. Love helps to heal just about everything.

41

By the time she's three, a kid knows what birthdays are all about. It's me-day. ALL ME. *My* presents, *my* friends, *my* cake—ME!!!

The great day can't come fast enough—and then it's over.

The downside of me-day is . . . it takes 365 "sleeps" to come again.

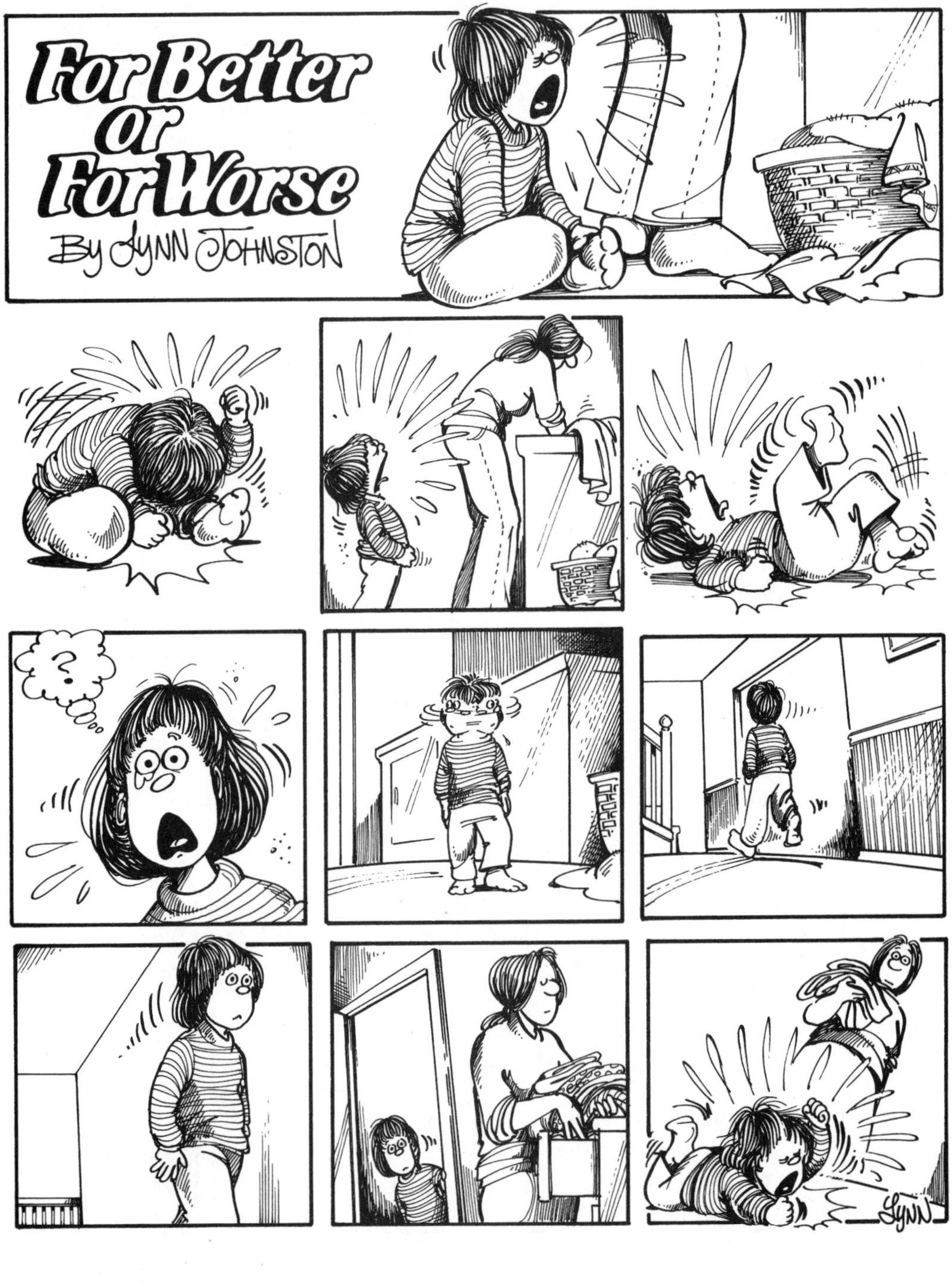

For Better or For Worse
By Lynn Johnston
?
Lynn

There's no point in being the youngest if you can't get all of the attention most of the time. April was a tantrum specialist. She knew when and how to throw one; she'd had practice.

The most successful tantrums are thrown in public places where Mom or Dad do not want to appear (A.) permissive or (B.) a bad parent. A good tantrum begins with a whine: "I wannaaah" or "I don't wannaaah," using just the right tone, just the right expression. Once the target audience has acknowledged that a problem exists, sit down if you're on foot or rock wildly back and forth if you're riding. Continue to whine. Within seconds this will result in some gently soothing encouragement, soon followed by rumbling commands and then possibly—a bargaining stance. "If you can be good for just a short while longer (fill in the blank) will happen!" Weigh the peace offering. Start again, this time with higher decibels and copious tears. Another bargaining pitch, "If you don't stop that immediately, I am going to (fill in the blank)!!!!" Consider the consequences and carry on.

The artful tantrum is often performed face down on any surface that can be slapped or pounded (avoid small stones and sand). The roll-over-and-kick method's good too.

By working both limbs and lungs to the max, you should succeed in creating enough anxiety to force your victims to (A.) take you home or (B.) put you to bed. Either way the result will be a well-earned nap—which is what you needed in the first place. April knew, if nothing else, that a tantrum was good exercise.

Big brothers are very useful. They can teach you how to burp the alphabet, how to spit sideways, and how to eat a slice of baloney and leave the skin. Michael Patterson took his role seriously. He knew his little sister would pick up all kinds of gross habits . . . so she might as well learn them at home.

To a woman, hair is of ultimate importance. It's an expression of her individuality, her temperament, her self.

To kids and animals, it's something that grows back.

47

April knew how to open the gate in the fence that separated her yard from the yard next door. Once, when she left the gate open, the Pattersons' dog, Farley, wandered over to visit the neighbors' dog, Sera. The result was a litter of pups born nine weeks later!

April always wondered what she had to do with it.

The bigger April grew, the more she could do, and John became increasingly close to his youngest child. He taught her how to fish, fly kites, and make castles in the sand—and of the two parents, he was the most likely to "give in."

Mom, on the other hand, meant business. If she asked April to clean up her room, she had to at least try. If Mom said no dessert until the peas were gone, April disposed of the peas. If Mom asked for some help with the laundry, it meant peas had been found in a pocket.

It was harder to "get around" Mom.

When Sera and Farley's pups were born, everyone came to see them. April had never seen a brand-new baby of any kind and wanted to play with them all. Connie told her that the pups were too small to play with, but that she could watch them and in a few weeks they'd be old enough to handle.

The puppies were smooth and dark with flat pink noses. April watched them nurse from their mother. Elly told her that she had once nursed like that too! "Like that?!!" she asked, pointing to Sera. "No, from me." Elly replied, laughing.

Sera's babies grew fast. April and Elizabeth went to see them every day. Soon, the puppies' colors changed, and so did the shapes of their faces.

One little black and tan pup seemed friendlier that all the rest and the two girls asked if they could take him home. "Pleeeeeease," April pleaded. ". . . oh, pleeeease?"

For Better or For Worse
By Lynn Johnston

YOU KNOW, EL... THE POEMS AND THE SONGS ARE ALL WRONG...

THIS IS PUPPY LOVE!!!

$\mathcal{E}$dgar the puppy grew and adapted to life at the Patterson house. He ran rings around his father, Farley, who was getting to be quite an old dog.

Early one spring, Elly and John announced they were taking a vacation alone, and that Grandma Carrie would be coming to hold down the fort while they were away. April was almost five.

Grandma Carrie, John's mother, had spent most of her life working on a farm, just outside Winnipeg, Manitoba. Now retired, she and Grandpa Will looked forward to visits with the grandchildren. This was the first time she'd come to Ontario alone.

Tall and slender with gray-green eyes and soft white hair, Carrie Patterson took over the household as if she'd always been there. She liked baking and hiking, picking berries and chipping wood. She kept binoculars on the windowsill so she could watch the birds. April learned to identify chickadees and finches, robins and jays. Carrie loved having a youngster around who learned fast and was eager to please.

Together, they'd take the dogs for a run in the ravine behind the

house. "You're not to come down here alone," said Carrie, "not ever, do you understand?" April said she did. It was something she'd been told before.

When Elly and John came home, they were full of stories about the cruise they had taken. They spread photos on the dining room table and April felt ignored. She went out into the backyard where she found a small toy boat. There was a river at the bottom of the ravine. Maybe it would float! April knew she was never to go down to the river alone, so she kept her promise. The dogs went with her.

AAAAHHH!
COUGH COUGH
MA-MAAA

GASP!!

SOMETHING'S WRONG—I KNOW IT!

RUN, DEAR!—I'LL WAIT HERE.

WHAT'S GOING ON, DAD?

APRIL'S MISSING, LIZ—HAVE YOU SEEN HER?

YEAH—I SAW HER AWHILE AGO... PLAYING WITH A TOY BOAT!

A TOY BOAT?!

APRIL!!

APRIL, CAN YOU TAKE MY HAND? —I CAN'T REACH HER, ELLY!!

GRAB THAT BRANCH—I'LL HOLD YOUR JACKET!!

PLEASE...IF I NEVER DO ANYTHING ELSE IN MY WHOLE LIFE.... LET ME DO THIS!!!

HERE, LET'S WRAP HER UP IN MY SWEATER BEFORE SHE FREEZES.

SHE IS PRETTY COLD.

I'M SORRY, DADDY!—MOM WAS LOOKING AT BOAT PICTURES, AN' I FOUND A BOAT INNA YARD, AN' I WANTED TO SAIL IT INNA RIVER, BUT I SLIPPED AN' FELL IN!!

HONEY, YOU KNOW YOU'RE NOT SUPPOSED TO GO DOWN TO THE RIVER!—IF IT WASN'T FOR FARLEY, YOU WOULDN'T BE HERE!

YES, IF IT WASN'T FOR FARLEY...

DADDY?

ELLY, WHY DON'T YOU AND MOM TAKE APRIL UP TO THE HOUSE AND GET WARM...I'LL BE THERE IN A MINUTE.

DADDY....

HEY, FARLEY! WHAT'S THE MATTER, OLD BOY? WHAT'S THE MATTER?!!

DADDY.....HE ISN'T BREATHING!!

After her rescue from the river, April was quickly taken up to the house. She didn't know that the dog that had fought so hard to save her had died. It was Grandma Carrie who told her. "This was his greatest gift," she said. "Farley loved you enough to give his life for you. We have so much to be thankful for."

Still, April knew she was responsible. It was her fault. If only she hadn't gone down to the river, Farley would still be here. "If only I'd stayed in the garden! If only I'd done what I was told!" Her head filled with "if onlys."

They buried him beside a tree on the hillside: a tall, graceful maple. It's now called "Farley's tree." It's a quiet, peaceful place were April often goes to be alone.

Now and then, she hears a familiar sound, something like dog paws shuffling through the leaves. And the ache comes back, along with the memory.

The lessons that stay with you forever are usually the ones that were the hardest learned.

When Michael went to university and moved out of the house, April got a room of her own. This didn't keep her from slipping back into her sister's room—if just for the joy of hearing her holler. Elizabeth was turning into a young woman and wanted her privacy. April felt lonely and wanted Elizabeth.

There were times it was great to be "littlest." Being ten years younger than her sister meant phone calls to listen in on. Elizabeth didn't mind taking April to the ice cream shop or a Saturday matinee, but she was a teenager now, with a life of her own. Whenever she put her jacket on to go out in the evening, April knew she'd be excluded from Elizabeth's world and left at home.

Michael was a full fifteen years older and more like a parent than a brother. He tossed her about the way Dad did and when he learned to drive, Elly trusted him to take April to school or the park.

Most of the kids in the neighborhood had grown up with Elizabeth and Michael. Few younger families had moved in, so what April missed most of all were kids to play with—someone her own age.

HOWCOME I CAN'T GO WIF LIVABEFF?

SHE WANTS TO BE WITH HER FRIENDS, APRIL.

WHERE'S MICHAEL?

DOWN TOWN.—THEY HAVE THEIR OWN INTERESTS, HONEY. THEY CAN'T ALWAYS TAKE YOU WITH THEM!

ARE YOU EVER GONNA HAVE ANOTHER BABY, MOM?

I DON'T THINK SO, APRIL. ...WHY?

I WANNA BE **BIGGER** THAN SOMEONE!

In day care, Becky McGuire and Duncan Anderson became April's closest friends. Becky, like April, was an "only" child surrounded at home by grownups. Duncan had a brother, Charles, who was two years older, making him a bit more accommodating than the two girls were.

Having friends was important. April loved to be with them . . . but April's world was still home.

For Better or For Worse
By Lynn Johnston

Pre-kindergarten opened the door to big kids' school! Pre-K meant rules and order and serious stuff. It meant cooperation and remembering and getting things right. It also meant new grown-ups to get used to, which was always interesting. They all have their weak spots, and kids tend to find them . . . fast!

A B C D E F GEE H I J K ELLEMENNO PEEE

TODAY, WE ARE SHARING OUR COLORS! REMEMBER TO SHARE.

WHEW! WHEN YOU GET INTO PRE-K...THEY REALLY MAKE YOU **WORK!**

HOW HIGH CAN YOU JUMP, BECKY? I CAN JUMP DIS HIGH!

HOW FAST CAN YOU RUN? I CAN RUN REALLY, REALLY, REALLY, REALLY REALLY FAST!!

... CAN I TRY YOUR SHOES?

BECKY, IF WE'RE GONNA TRADE SHOES, WHY DON'T WE TRADE JACKETS! OK!

IF WE TRADE JACKETS, WHY DON'T WE TRADE SHIRTS?! YAH!

... AN' IF WE'RE GONNA TRADE SHIRTS....

Lynn

67

$\mathcal{B}$ecky McGuire was slightly built with blue eyes and pale blonde hair. She had freckles and one tooth missing on the bottom, she was chatty and was allergic to stuff, and whenever they played games, Becky wanted to be first.

They met on the first day of pre-K because of alphabetical order. Since there were no "Ns" or "Os" in the class, M came before P and the two girls were made to share a table.

At first they bickered. Both were aggressive and used to being number one. They seemed to be evenly matched, however, and soon realized that united, they could have a lot more fun.

Duncan Anderson was a shy little boy. He had dark skin and dark eyes, and a grin that endeared him to everyone. Although he willingly took part in games and activities, he seemed to stay on the outside looking in.

April felt safe with Duncan. He was easy to be with. He'd stand up for himself but always walked away from a fight. Duncan and Becky were opposites—and April fit right into the middle.

April's world was expanding now. She had friends and a life outside the family. She was adapting to bus rides and teachers, new rules, and playground politics.

Kindergarten was not just a place where you learned from books, it was also a place where you learned about people—and where on the playground you fit in.

For Better or For Worse
By Lynn Johnston

GIDDY-UP, DADDY! GIDDY-UP! GIDDY-UP!

NEIGHHHH SNORT WHINNY NEIGHHHHHHH

THUMPITY SHUFFLE SLAP THUMP....

OW

HI-YO SLIVER! AWAAAAYYYY

VERY FUNNY.

KNOW WHAT, LIVABEFF? WHEN I'M AS BIG AS YOU, I'M GONNA ASK FOR A HORSE! - A REAL ONE!!

OH, YEAH?

YAH! I'M GONNA HAVE A HORSE AN' BEFORE I GET A HORSE, DO YOU KNOW WHAT ELSE I'M GONNA GET?

WHAT?

I'M GONNA GET A PUPPY, A KITTY, A BIRDIE, A HANGSTER, A TURTLE, A GUINEA PIG, A BUNNY....

....RATS!

YOU'RE NOT GOING TO TAKE YOUR COWBOY HAT TO BED, ARE YOU, APRIL?

I WANT TO!!

YOU'RE TAKING YOUR VEST AND BOOTS, TOO?

UH HUH.

WELL, OK, HONEY! - BUT, I'LL BE DARNED IF I KNOW WHY!

....YOU NEVER KNOW WHEN YOU'RE GOING TO DREAM ABOUT HORSES.

Elly and John began to see their youngest child blossom. She had ideas and abilities and dreams they had never known about. And April, whose world was a mix of what's real and what isn't, believed that seeds became flowers and dreams can come true.

KNOW WHAT I'M GONNA GET WHEN I GROW UP? I'M GONNA GET A **HORSE**! A **REAL** ONE!!

HE'S GONNA BE **DIS** HIGH, AN' HE'S GONNA RUN FASTER THAN **ANYFING**!

AN' HE'S GONNA BE BROWN WIF WHITE ON HIS FACE AN' HE'S GONNA BE **BEAUTIFUL**!

WHATCHA GONNA CALL HIM?

I DUNNO. I HAVEN'T DREAMED THAT FAR YET.

COME ON, APRIL. I'LL GIVE YOU A HORSIE RIDE. WHERE DO YOU WANT TO GO?

ANYWHERE! FAST! GO FAST! GO FAST!

FASTER! FASTER! FASTER! FAST!!

OOHH! GASP! ... I GOTTA SIT DOWN!

AREN'T I S'POSED TO GET OFF FIRST?

For Better or For Worse

HAH! I CAN'T BELIEVE HOW **DUMB** THESE OLD HORROR MOVIES ARE!!

LOOK AT THE WAY THE MONSTER'S EYEBALL FALLS OUT, MAN! —YOU JUST **KNOW** IT'S PLASTIC!

YEAH, RIGHT! AS IF SOME GUY IS GONNA BE ABLE TO WALK AROUND WITHOUT A **HEAD!**

AN', THIS IS TOO MUCH! LIKE, WE ARE SUPPOSED TO BELIEVE THAT'S A **TENTACLE**? ... GET SOME REALISTIC SLIME! OK, GUYS?!!!

CLICK!

That space in a child's life when the tooth fairy, goblins, and Santa exist is all too short a time. Elly and John treasured each moment, knowing that April would soon begin to question everything— and the only acceptable answers would be the truth.

For Better or For Worse

By Lynn Johnston

OK, APRIL, BEFORE YOU GET STARTED, I WANT TO SHOW YOU SOMETHING!

NOW, THE FIRST THING YOU GOTTA LEARN IS THE SNOWPLOW. POINT YOUR SKIS LIKE THIS, SO THEY LOOK LIKE A TRIANGLE...

APRIL, LISTEN TO ME!

DON'T YOU WANT TO LEARN HOW TO STOP?

NO!

FOOMP!

...NOW I WANT TO LEARN HOW TO STOP.

$\mathcal{B}$y four and a half (halves are very important), April could ride a bicycle, tie her own shoes, and put a big jacket on all by herself. She had chores to do, like feeding the dog and taking her plate from the table.

There was homework from school and now April would call Becky on the phone to discuss it—just like Elizabeth.

There was a tape measure glued to the kitchen door. She had grown two inches since the last time! Dad marked the new height with black pen. It was like one of those "donation thermometers" you see at the mall. And April's goal was BIG!

She was allowed to sleep over at Becky's house and to have an aquarium downstairs. Snakes and bugs and injured birds found their way into the Patterson house—and, with a little unskilled veterinary care—found their way out again.

Though April could swim now and make her own sandwich . . . even though she knew how to spell stuff, could add and subtract . . . even though she slept with the light off and had completely stopped sucking her thumb, she still clung tightly to Elly.

Independence depends so much on Mom!

What is the matter with parents? Why do they have to go away on their own? What could they possibly do that wouldn't be more fun with me around?

The explanation that they need a "rest" from their children is never quite good enough, especially when you're almost a grown-up . . . "almost" five.

Spending a week or two with another family is educational. Everyone does things differently.

Becky's house was different, the food was different, and so were the rules. Spending a week or two with Becky was wonderful. Once again, it made April appreciate "home."

Four is an excellent birthday. It's better than three and seriously better than two. Five is the number to be. It's one whole hand with all the fingers. It's halfway, exactly, to ten. Five is when you can have a real party where nobody throws up or wets their pants—or at least is embarrassed if they do so.

Five is cool. It means the very next year, you'll be in grade one. It means loose teeth and an allowance and being tall enough to go on some fairground rides that say, "nobody allowed below this line."

Five is when grown-ups ask you a question and listen to the answer. It's how old Dennis the Menace has been—for his whole life! But . . . it's young enough to still be "baby." Yes, it's a wonderful thing to be five.

For Better or For Worse

By Lynn Johnston

"NOW", SAID BAKER BOB, "THESE PIES NEED NUTMEG AND CINNAMON!"

SCRATCH

SCRATCH & SNIFF

BAKER BOB'S BIG BANQUET

"BUT, WHAT ABOUT THE MAPLE TARTS?" SAID HELPER SAM.

SNIFFFF

"THESE POPOVERS ARE PERFECT!" CRIED THE MAYOR, "AND THE FLAN IS FABULOUS!" SAID HIS WIFE.

SCRATCH... SNIFF

AND, FROM THAT DAY ON, EVERYONE SAID THAT BAKER BOB WAS THE BEST BAKER IN THE BUSINESS.

SNIFF SNUFF SNIFF

SCRATCH...SNIFF... SCRATCH... -LICK!

LICK, LICK... SCRATCH, LICK SLUPPP... MUNCH!

BAKER BOB'S BIG

MFFF SMACK... ...BLEAH!

6

80

WHEN I GROW UP, I'M GONNA GO EVERYWHERE IN THE WORLD!

YEAH?

I WANNA SEE THE COLDEST PLACES AN' THE HOTTEST PLACES! I WANNA SEE ICE-BERGS AN' JUNGLES AN' LIONS AN' GIRAFFES AN' PENGUINS AN' KANGAROOS AN' WHALES!!

THAT WOULD BE COOL, APRIL.

LIVABEFF, I GOT A QUESTION.

WHAT'S THAT?

... WILL ALL THOSE THINGS STILL BE AROUND WHEN I GET THERE?

MOM.... I NEED A HUGGY.

LOTSA HUGGIES! MORE! LOTS AN' LOTSAN!

DON'T LET GO. NOT YET.... DON'T LET GO.....

OK, THAT'S ENOUGH. YOU CAN STOP!

...I'M FULL NOW!!

WHATCHA DOING IN MICHAEL'S ROOM, LIVABEFF?

NOTHING. JUST LOOKING AROUND.

I CAN'T WAIT 'TIL HE COMES HOME! I WANT TO SHOW HIM THE BIKE I GOT FOR MY BIRFDAY! I GOT LOTSA STUFF TO TELL HIM!—I CAN'T **WAIT!!**

DO YOU MISS HIM WHEN HE'S AWAY, LIVABEFF?

YEAH—BUT IF YOU TELL HIM, YOU'RE TOAST!

I GUESS THAT MEANS SHE WANTS ME TO TELL.

For Better or For Worse

By Lynn Johnston

OH!

DADDY, I TRIED AN' I TRIED, BUT I CAN'T DO IT!

HERE, HONEY... LET ME GIVE YOU A HAND.

I'LL HOLD ON TIGHT, AND YOU PEDAL!

IT'S OK! I'VE GOT YOU!

DADDY, I **DID** IT! I RODE A TWO-WHEEL BIKE ALL BY MYSELF!! —AN' YOU KNOW WHAT?—IT WAS **EASY!**

I KNOW...

THE HARD PART WAS LETTING GO.

HOW COME YOUR DOG'S CALLED "EDGAR"?

'CAUSE HE GROWLS ALLA TIME. YOU KNOW.... "ED-GRRR".

LOTSA PEOPLE GIVE THEIR DOGS FUNNY NAMES 'CAUSE OF THE THINGS THEY DO. —RIGHT, LIZ?

YEAH.

WE KNOW A GUY WHO CALLED HIS DOG "AROO" BE-CAUSE HE HOWLED A LOT—AND AN-OTHER GUY WHO CALLS HIS DOGS "DIGBY AN' PUDDLES"!

I WONDER WHAT WE'D BE CALLED IF MOM NAMED **US** LIKE THAT!!

...I PREFER NOT TO THINK ABOUT IT.

MOM, DOES BECKY HAFTA GO HOME? CAN'T SHE SLEEP OVER?

NOT TONIGHT, HONEY.

PLEASE, MOM? APRIL, BECKY STAYED HERE LAST WEEK-END, YOU STAYED AT HER HOUSE ON MONDAY, AND THEN SHE WAS HERE FOR SUPPER YESTERDAY AND TODAY!

YOU'RE JUST LIKE A COUPLE OF SISTERS!

WE ARE **NOT!**

...I'M NOT **TIRED** OF HER YET!!!

WHY DOES EDGAR SNIFF SO MUCH?

THAT'S WHAT ANIMALS DO, APRIL.

SNORF

DOGS HAVE A VERY KEEN SENSE OF SMELL. BY SNIFF-ING THINGS, THEY CAN TELL IF THERE'S FOOD AROUND OR IF ANOTHER DOG HAS BEEN ON THEIR TERRITORY.

IN FACT, HE CAN EVEN IDEN-TIFY YOU BY THE WAY YOU SMELL—BECAUSE EACH OF US HAS OUR OWN PARTICULAR ODOR!

WE DO?

SNIFF?

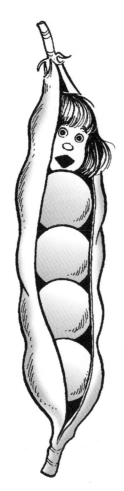

Dirt is good. You can dig in it, turn it into mud, build stuff with it, find bugs and rocks in it, and if you plant seeds or bulbs or even a piece of potato in dirt, something will grow. You've got to wait a while, but eventually a green shoot will curl its way up through the rich, brown particles and be something! Dirt is magical!

Elly has a garden at the back of the house. Except for the times she's added manure to the mix, she's managed to keep the dog out of it. April wasn't as easy to train. She loved the smell and the feel of dirt—especially when she was dressed to go out somewhere . . . and was wearing white.

She was soon given a small garden of her own. Grandma Marian sent her a set of tools and some seeds. The seeds grew and April couldn't wait to harvest the things she'd grown herself. For her, it was a good education, and a breakthrough in discipline. Not only did she show more respect for her mother's garden, April, now willingly, ate peas.

For Better or For Worse
By Lynn Johnston

No, April, you're too small to go on the big rollercoaster.

Please?!!

I AM **NOT**! — I AM NOT TOO SMALL! I WANNA GO ONNA **BIG** ONE! I WANNA **GO**!

Here's one you can ride. ...Let's try this one.

CHEEKY CHOO-CHOO

Guess what, Dad! Mom let me go onna big roller coaster... ALL BY MYSELF!!

For Better or For Worse

By Lynn Johnston

KNOW WHAT, MOM? KNOW WHAT WE DID TODAY? WE MADE A SOLAR SYSTEM WIF A BIG MELON INNA MIDDLE FOR THE SUN, AN' ALL OF THE PLANETS WERE MADE FROM FRUITS!... BUT, WE NEVER GOT FINISHED, 'CAUSE STUART GORMAN ATE THE GRAPE THAT WAS S'POSED TO BE PLUTO!

AN' KNOW WHAT? DANICA? THE GIRL WIF THE HORSE? SHE FREW UP AT LUNCH 'CAUSE NATHAN PUT A BUG IN HIS MOUTH! —AN' KNOW WHAT?..

KNOW WHAT WE DID TODAY? A MAN CAME TO THE LIBRARY, AN' HE SHOWED US A VIDEO ABOUT STARS!

AN' HE SAID THE SUN WAS A STAR, BUT JANET SAID IT WASN'T AN' KNOW WHAT? JANET GOTS A TOOTH SHE CAN PUSH AROUND WIF HER TONGUE! NATHAN SAID HE SWALLOWED A TOOTH ONCE!!

IF YOU SWALLOWED A TOOTH... COULD IT BITE YOU ONNA STOMACH? HOW WOULD THE TOOTH FAIRY FIND IT?!!

JAMES SAID HE SAW THE TOOTH FAIRY ONCE, HE SAID SHE HAD REALLY, REALLY BAD BREATH! AN' KNOW WHAT? KNOW WHAT, MOM?

YACK, YACK, YACK YACK YACK YACK YACK YACK...

HI, MELBA, SORRY WE'RE A LITTLE LATE... I HAD TO GET APRIL FROM THE LIBRARY.

WELL, HELLO THERE!

I'M AMAZED, ELLY......IS SHE **ALWAYS** THIS QUIET?!

Big sisters are a pain. They tell you what to do, get mad if you touch their stuff, and they don't want you around sometimes. So why is it so lonely when they go away? Maybe it's because you can only go without teasing and arguing for a short period of time. It seems that kids need teasing and arguing as much as they need their good-night hugs.

One summer, Elizabeth went away to work on their cousin's farm. She came home carrying a white rabbit in a cage. It was a big, white flop-eared bunny and April was instantly in love! They called him Sheldon F. Bunsworthy (Mr. "B" for short!).

It was neat to have a new pet in the family—but having her big sister home was even better.

That year, April looked forward to starting kindergarten. This was as close to being in actual grade one as you could get! She took the big kids' bus to H.G. Davis Public School and stood in line beside the west wing the way they told her to on introduction day—the day she went with Mom. Now she was on her own.

There were kids she knew from pre-K and some parents, too. There were new kids, shy kids, silly kids, happy kids, and one who just ran back and forth between the bike racks and the wall.

There were kids whose families had emigrated from India, Pakistan, Lebanon, and China. There were kids from Hungary, Poland, Italy, South America, and the Caribbean. There were kids from first nations whose ancestors lived here long before the fur trade began. Kids with different names, other languages, different games.

But today, they were all exactly the same. They were all starting kindergarten at the very same time at the very same school. Today, they were classmates.

EVERYBODY'S STANDING UP AN' SAYING THEIR NAMES IN FRONT OF THE CLASS.

IT'S ALMOST MY TURN... ALMOST... ALMOST.... I'M NEXT!

ERK!
MY NAME IS APRIL PATTERSON!!

SOMETIMES YOU GOTTA GET WORDS OUT FAST ... OR THEY WON'T COME OUT AT ALL!

LISTEN, EVERYONE — I'VE DIVIDED OUR CLASS INTO 6 GROUPS!

EACH GROUP HAS 4 PEOPLE IN IT, AND EACH GROUP IS REPRESENTED BY A DIFFERENT COLOR.

WHAT GROUP ARE YOU IN?

BLUE GROUP!

ME TOO!

THIS IS COOL, DUNCAN. — WE'RE BOTH THE SAME COLOR!!

THIS IS A NEAT PLAYGROUND, APRIL! IT'S WAY BIGGER THAN THE ONE WE HAD IN PRE-K!

AN' THERE'S MORE SWINGS, TOO!

LOOK! THESE ARE THE **GOOD** SWINGS, BECKY! THESE ARE THE COMFTRABLE ONES!!!

YOU KNOW IT'S A GOOD SCHOOL WHEN THEY GOT GOOD SWINGS!

AN' GOOD TEACHERS!

ESPECIALLY THE ONES WITH THE BIG WIDE SEATS!!

SO, HOW WAS YOUR FIRST WEEK IN KINDERGARTEN, APRIL?

AWESOME!

WE'RE ALL IN COLOR GROUPS AN' WE DO GAMES, AN' WE DO STUFF ON THE COMPUTERS AN' WE HAVE SONGS AN' PUZZLES AN' STORIES.

WELL, IT SOUNDS LIKE FUN TO ME!!

YEAH, BUT YOU KNOW WHAT, DAD?

...I THINK THEY'RE TRYING TO FOOL US INTO LEARNING SOMETHING!

When you get to be almost six, there's one word you start to hear over and over again: "responsibility."

It's your responsibility to clean your room. Looking after a pet is your responsibility. Sharing stuff isn't just the right thing to do; when you're older it's a responsibility!

It's really, really nice to be big. It's just too bad that growing up means having so much . . . responsibility.

YOU REALLY MEAN IT? YOU'RE REALLY GONNA GIVE YOUR BUNNY TO ME?

UH HUH. HE'S ALL YOURS.

OH, WOW! DID YOU HEAR THAT, MR.B? YOU BELONG TO ME NOW!!

THAT MEANS YOU HAFTA FEED HIM AN' CLEAN HIS CAGE FROM NOW ON.

I WILL!

BUT I CAN STILL PLAY WITH HIM WHEN-EVER I WANT TO.

OK!

THANKS, 'LIZABETH!

HEY... I JUST WANTED TO DO YOU A FAVOR.

BYE! - SEE YOU LATER!!

I HOPE THE BUS COMES SOON. I GOT A TURTLE IN MY BACK-PACK.

APRIL!

WHAT'S HE IN?

I PUT HIM IN A BOTTLE WITH HOLES IN, AN' THEN I PUT HIM IN A LUNCH BAG.

WELL, I HOPE HE'S OK WHEN HE GETS OUT.

WHAT'S THAT FOR?

APRIL'S TURTLES.

TURTLES?!

THEY'RE BECKY'S, BUT SHE GAVE THEM TO ME! - COOL, HUH?

MOM SAID SINCE I WAS LOOKING AFTER THE BUNNY SO WELL, SHE'D LET ME HAVE THE TURTLES!

BUT THE SCOTTS GAVE YOU A FISH LAST WEEK!

MAN, WE NEVER HAD ALL THIS STUFF IN OUR HOUSE BEFORE!

'TIS THE AGE OF AQUARIUMS.

Waiting for something wonderful to happen is really hard to do. Sometimes, grownups make kids wait for stuff—just to make the experience more enjoyable. They say they want the moment to "last longer."

Grownups forget that for somebody small . . . a moment can last forever.

MOM .... I WANNA TELL YOU SOMETHING.

I'M SORRY, APRIL. IT'S IMPOLITE TO WHISPER THINGS IN FRONT OF OTHER PEOPLE.

IF YOU HAVE SOMETHING TO SAY, YOU SHOULD SAY IT OUT LOUD.

BUT...

WELL?

I'M BORED, THE SOUP IS GROSS, AND I WANNA GO HOME!

What's big and what's small? When it comes to growing up, age and size and what's expected of you can be confusing.

April was intuitive and could express herself well. She learned quickly and was often trusted to do things on her own.

At home, she lived in a world of adults, which was reflected in her mannerisms and vocabulary. "You're a big girl now," they told her, but her spirit and her emotions were of someone small. The admonition, "You're too old to do that!" might just as easily be followed by "You can't do that, you're not old enough!"

She'd stand and look in the mirror, wondering if she was pretty. She searched in her closet for cool stuff to wear and she talked on the phone, sprawled on the couch, the way her sister did. Still, she was afraid of the dark, believed in fairies, and when things went wrong, she'd sit down, right where she was and cry—the way anybody would who was almost six.

What April learned was: sometimes it's nice to be big and sometimes it's nice to be small. It all depends on your audience.

For Better or For Worse
By Lynn Johnston

OH, LIZ! HE'S ADORABLE!!

LOOK AT HIM! HE'S SO CUTE!

AWW!

IS THIS GORDON AND TRACEY'S NEW BABY?

UH HUH.

MOM AN' I ARE LOOKING AFTER HIM TODAY! HIS NAME IS PAUL.

WHAT'S THE MATTER, APRIL?

NUFFING.

ARE YOU A LITTLE JEALOUS OF THE NEW BABY?

I DUNNO

WELL, THE GIRLS MAY BE MAKING A FUSS OVER HIM 'CAUSE HE'S SO LITTLE ... BUT, HE CAN'T DO ANY OF THE THINGS THAT YOU CAN DO!!

YOU'RE 6! YOU CAN TALK AND READ AND SING! YOU CAN SWIM AND COUNT AND RIDE A BIKE—SO, COMPARED TO A BRAND NEW BABY—YOU'RE EXTRA SPECIAL!

OH.

Z

Michael Patterson went away to university. It wasn't a temporary thing. He actually moved out of the house and took his bed with him. For his younger sister, this meant two things: "A room for friends to sleep in!" and "When will I see you again?"

The time she spent with him now meant more than ever.

For Better or For Worse
By Lynn Johnston

APRIL!!!

APRIL, DID YOU LET THE RABBIT GET UP ON MY BED AGAIN?

WELL.

WAIT! DON'T THROW THAT OUT!

WHY NOT?

MICHAEL SAYS THEY'RE RABBIT SEEDS. HE SAYS IF YOU PLANT THEM, YOU CAN GROW RABBITS!

OH, COME ON, YOU DON'T BELIEVE THAT, DO YOU?

MICHAEL SAID SO. HE SAID IT WAS THE ACTUAL TRUTH!

AN' WHEN IT GETS WARM ENOUGH OUTSIDE, I'M GONNA PLANT SOME, AN' GET MORE RABBITS.

APRIL... YOU'RE NOT SAVING THOSE, ARE YOU?

GRASS SEED

Family comes first! Then, it's friends and pets. Or is it pets before friends? Anyway—April's dog, rabbit, fish, and foundlings have always been there when she needed them.

There's comfort in talking to an animal whose eyes seem to tell you they fully understand. She could talk to Becky, but Becky didn't listen like her bunny did—and Becky had secrets and ideas and troubles of her own to share.

It was the pets April turned to when she was in one of those "I'm feeing grouchy and strange"... and "I don't know how to explain it" kind of moods.

When you're with animals ... you don't have to say a thing.

It was summertime again: her favorite time of year. April was enrolled in swimming lessons and summer ballet. There was baseball in the park and on weekends, her dad took her fishing! There were plans to drive to Prince Edward Island and maybe even go camping . . .

She didn't understand the severity of the phone call from Grandpa Jim. When Elly announced she would be going to Vancouver to see her mother, April was happy to be going too.

An airplane ride with Mom! A chance to see cousins she'd only met once before. Even Her Uncle Phil would be there. It all sounded like a party—but it wasn't.

Elly explained that Grandma Marian was going to have a serious operation. It was something to do with her heart. Grandma hadn't been well for some time and everyone was worried—so April tried to worry too.

It was a clear, sunny day when they landed. The mountains were spectacular. The drive to the North Shore took them past Stanley Park and over the Lion's Gate Bridge. April absorbed the scenery, only half listening as Mom and Grandpa talked quietly in the front of the car.

While April played with cousins Jaime and Grant, Grandma was in surgery. Hushed conversations between grown-ups were largely ignored by the three children, but April went to bed at night with an ache inside, and no pets to cuddle.

When they were finally allowed into the hospital to see her, the children thought Grandma looked different. Even though she smiled and reached out to them, she wasn't the same. She looked small in the bed: fragile and childlike. For the first time, April sensed she was stronger than someone older than she was. She knew now that life didn't last forever, and was afraid of what was to come.

Serious things can be set aside when you're six. You can immerse yourself in a world where fantasy and reality constantly merge and separate. Grown-ups watching may think you're unaware of things that go on around you—but that's not true. Make-believe isn't "child's play" . . . it's an art.

Real fighting rarely occurs in the Patterson household, but every now and then, a bickering session seems to clear the air. Strange how things happen when everyone involved just needs a few good hugs.

Grade one is major! Grade one is like climbing over a fence you've been looking through for a long time . . . and on the other side is the future.

Grade one is for real. It's the first rung on the ladder to somewhere! It's deadlines and homework and following rules. After six years of testing others, April was about to test herself. She was ready.

She had new pencils and scissors, a ruler, eraser, and pens. The smell of new books, the excited chatter of friends and the feel of a desk that would be hers for almost a year made the first moments of the first day better than anything.

For the first week, she called her teacher "Dad," but that was OK—everyone did. Until now, their teachers had been women, and Mr. Rose was a surprise.

He was pretty old, maybe 30. He called his students "ladies and gentlemen." He used stories and games and pictures and films to explain things. He was strict, but he was funny and fair.

April learned a lot in grade one, because learning is fun—but mostly because of Mr. Rose. She was lucky to have him for her first year.

Someone who loves to teach can teach you to love learning.

In some ways her teacher and her dad were super heroes . . .but real ones use secret weapons and disguises.

FOR Better OR FOR WORSE

By Lynn Johnston

WHY ARE PEOPLE SELLING POPPIES TODAY, MOM?

THEY'RE A SYMBOL, APRIL. SOMETHING TO MAKE US REMEMBER.

A MAN CALLED JOHN McCRAE WROTE A BEAUTIFUL POEM ABOUT THE POPPIES THAT GREW IN FLANDERS FIELDS.

ALSO IN THE FIELDS WERE CROSSES, MARKING THE GRAVES OF SOLDIERS WHO DIED FIGHTING THE WAR.

WHY DO I HAFTA WEAR A POPPY?!

I'M NOT REALLY SURE WHAT A WAR IS!

I KNOW.

AND THAT, I THINK, IS THE BEST REASON OF ALL!

LEST WE FORGET

GET AWAY FROM ME, APRIL!

HOWCOME?

'CAUSE HEAD LICE CAN SPREAD TO OTHER PEOPLE! I DON'T WANNA CATCH WHAT YOU HAVE! — STAY AWAY!

RINGG

HELLO? UH, HI, ANTHONY....

OH, NOTHING. JUST BABY-SITTING MY LOUSY LITTLE SISTER.

MOM? HOWCOME I HAD BUGS IN MY HAIR?

WELL, IT SOMETIMES HAPPENS WHEN CHILDREN ARE IN BIG GROUPS, APRIL. THEY USUALLY PASS FROM ONE PERSON TO ANOTHER.

HAVEN'T THEY TOLD YOU ABOUT THESE THINGS IN SCHOOL?

NOT YET.

— BUT THEY **DID** TEACH US HOW TO SHARE!

GUESS WHAT, APRIL! — AFTER YOUR MOM TOLD THE TEACHER YOU HAD HEAD LICE — LOTS MORE KIDS HAD IT, TOO!

THEY'RE CHECKING EVERYONE IN THE SCHOOL, AN' WE HAFTA TAKE THIS PAPER HOME, THAT EXPLAINS WHAT TO DO!

MORE KIDS GOT IT, DUNCAN?

UH-HUH. BUT I THINK YOU WERE THE FIRST.

REALLY? COOL!!

THIS IS THE FIRST TIME I'VE EVER BEEN **FIRST** IN ANYTHING!!

Even super heroes have their bad days. The smallest thing can bring them to their knees.

For Sockhead, the enemy was bugs! An outbreak of head lice wasn't unusual. Kids got them in kindergarten and for weeks there would be spot checks and lectures on how to avoid them. April had managed to escape the villains until now.

Elly washed everything in the hottest water. Everyone in the family doused themselves with white stuff that smelled like camphor and had to be left on for 20 minutes. Neighbors avoided coming to the house and the school nurse suggested that April stay home for a day and asked to be "kept informed."

Surprisingly, April "itched to know more." John brought a microscope home from the clinic so she could see what the bugs looked like. She read about them and drew one for Elly to put on the fridge.

The word "lousy" now had meaning and grossing her sister out was cool! Every living thing was of interest to this six-year-old and John said maybe, some day, she'd be a veterinarian and April agreed.

After all, veterinarians can be super heroes . . . if you think about it.

MOM! MOM! MICHAEL'S HERE WITH HIS NEW GIRL-FRIEND!

I KNOW, APRIL.

*R*elationships between the boys and the girls were changing now. There were boys she "liked" and boys she didn't. ("Like"—meaning being attracted to.) She gossiped with Becky about how cute or uncute a guy was and they wondered if their teacher, Mr. Rose, ever dated.

When Michael came home with Deanna Sobinski, everyone knew she'd be part of the family, April looked at her and wondered how many times they'd kissed and if he'd said "I love you."

She knew a lot about love. She watched TV! She was starting to think about physical stuff-especially at swimming lessons, when everyone was almost (giggle) . . . naked.

She started to wonder where babies came from-for real, and she knew her mom would tell her, when she was ready.

But April wasn't ready yet. If it had anything to do with boys . . . she didn't want to know.

HIYA, SHORTSTUFF! HOW'S THE KID?

MICHAEL!

I'M ELIZABETH.

DEANNA SOBINSKI.

GREAT. THE FIRST INTRODUCTION HAS BEEN EASIER THAN I THOUGHT IT WOULD BE!

MICHAEL, ARE YOU TWO IN LOVE WIF EACH OTHER?

April had an allowance now. She got two dollars a week for doing chores. Sometimes, when she didn't do everything, she only got half and that was OK . . . except at Christmastime.

She was almost seven and had learned how to save. "If I work really hard, maybe I can buy a gift for everyone," she thought. By December she had saved twenty dollars: five dollars for each member of the family. It was the most money she'd ever made in her life!

Elly took her to Philpott's store and promised not to watch as April chose her gifts. She didn't ask for help when she chose things for Dad and Mike and Elizabeth. There was even a bit left over for Deanna and the dog.

This was the most amazing Christmas ever. For the first time, she was more

excited about the things she was giving than the things she got. It felt wonderful.

First-time things often do.

ll kinds of first-time things were happening. She won a skipping contest and learned how to dive. She put a worm in her mouth in front of some guys and everyone found out about it. She graduated to junior ballet and enrolled in skating lessons. She did 3-D computer games, used a calculator, and wrote to a kid in Australia.

Mom let her use the sewing machine even though she could hardly reach the pedal and a kid called Bradford said he'd give her a doughnut if she showed him stuff that was private. April said, "NO!" and ran to tell a grown-up. She knew it was wrong. (Besides, the doughnut had raisins.)

School was the best now. They did projects for science and projects for peace. People asked what she thought, and she really had answers. April was starting to think there was nothing she couldn't do, if she just put her mind to it!

WHAT'S THIS, LIZ?

IT'S CALLED A COMPASS, OK?

BUT... THERE'S TWO KINDS OF COMPASSES. ONE THAT POINTS AN' ONE THAT MAKES CIRCLES.

OH.

POINK!

THIS MUST BE THE ONE THAT POINTS!

She was old enough to understand words and numbers, and to know why earthquakes happen and where rivers begin. She knew where babies came from and what the world looks like from space, but some things made no sense at all, like "Why did Grandma Marian have to get sick again?" She asked Elizabeth, "What can we do?" and Elizabeth said, "Make cookies."

Everyone was tense after Grandpa called, especially April's mom. She said things she didn't mean and cried easily. Dad helped her pack and drove her to the airport, alone. When he returned, April asked him what would happen. Dad said, "I can't say," and that answered her question.

DADDY, WHEN'S MOM COMING HOME?

I DON'T KNOW, APRIL. IT ALL DEPENDS ON HOW YOUR GRANDMA IS.

BESIDES, WE'RE MANAGING QUITE WELL ON OUR OWN.

WE'RE KEEPING THE HOUSE TIDY, I'M DOING THE LAUNDRY AND ELIZABETH'S LEARNING HOW TO COOK!

I KNOW.

THAT'S WHY I WANNA KNOW WHEN MOM'S COMING HOME.

APRIL, DON'T KICK OFF YOUR BOOTS WHEN YOU COME IN. STAND THEM ON THE MAT BY THE DOOR!

STOP TELLING ME WHAT TO DO. YOU'RE NOT MY MOM.

WELL, I'M IN CHARGE WHILE SHE'S AWAY, SO MOVE THOSE BOOTS!

NO!

FINE. THEN I'M GONNA TELL DAD WHEN HE COMES HOME.

SO? I'LL TELL HIM YOU YELLED AT ME!

AND TO THINK I ONCE SCOFFED AT PEOPLE WHO PREFER PETS TO CHILDREN.

121

"Everything happens for a reason," Elizabeth said as she hugged April tight. But she couldn't think of a reason for this. Grandma's death was hard for both to comprehend. Nobody in the family had died before, "Except Farley," April thought.

Memories of that day at the riverside came back as clearly as if it had happened yesterday. She thought about how suddenly she'd lost her dog, and now she would never see her grandmother again.

Together, the two girls turned the pages of the old photo album looking for images of Grandma, for Farley— for sunny days when everyone was there, laughing, having fun.

April wondered if Grandma and Farley were together and Elizabeth said they probably were.

"Grandma never liked pets," April said, "but, in heaven, at least they won't shed."

After his wife died, Grandpa Jim came home with his daughter. He was in a state of confusion and disbelief. Elizabeth gave him her room and moved into the room that had been Michael's. A change of scene would do him good, he thought. He hoped he could be useful and he wondered if he'd ever laugh again.

GRAMPA... WHY DOES IT TAKE SO LONG TO BE BIG?

WELL, APRIL, I THINK TIME GOES MORE SLOWLY FOR PEOPLE YOUR AGE.

REALLY?

UH-HUH. IT DOESN'T SPEED UP UNTIL YOU'RE ABOUT 20 - AND BY THE TIME YOU'RE 40, THE YEARS GO FLYING BY!!

AND WHEN YOU'RE OLD? WELL... IT SORT OF SLOWS DOWN AGAIN.

HOW COME?

...SO WE CAN SEE THE WORLD THROUGH THE EYES OF OUR GRAND-CHILDREN.

WELL, WHERE HAVE YOU TWO BEEN?

AT THE PARK - AN' GUESS WHAT, THEY FIXED THE MERRY-GO-ROUND!

I HELD ON TIGHT, AN' GRAMPA PUSHED ME 'ROUND AN' ROUND AN' ROUND!

YOU DON'T LOOK TOO MERRY, DAD - DID YOU RUN OUT OF GAS?

OH, NO - I'VE GOT PLENTY OF GAS.

... I JUST DON'T HAVE MUCH ENERGY.

Grandpa Jim was the kind of grown-up who could see the world through a kid's eyes. He remembered being too short to see through windows and sitting at tables that came up to your chin. He loved silliness and stories and he played on the floor with the pets. He'd wanted a dog for years, and felt guilty when he said to himself, "Perhaps, I can have one now."

WELL, EDDY... SHOULD I RISK MY KING?

124

$\mathscr{M}$r. B., the rabbit, was lots of work. Always digging, always chewing, and when let out of his cage, he refused to give up his freedom for as long as possible. Elizabeth wasn't much help, but April thought Grandpa looked promising. (He was already walking the dog.)

AAAUGH!

MR. B. WON'T GO INTO HIS CAGE, ELIZABETH. AS SOON AS I GET CLOSE TO HIM, HE HOPS AWAY!

COME BACK HERE! IF YOU DON'T DO WHAT I SAY, YOU'RE GONNA BE IN BIG **TROUBLE!**

ANIMALS! — THEY'RE SO **STUPID!!**

NOW THE BUNNY IS UNDER THE COUCH-AN' HE WON'T COME OUT!!

KNOW WHAT YOU SHOULD DO, APRIL? LIE ON THE FLOOR AN' ACT LIKE A CARROT!

LIKE THIS?

PERFECT!

THANKS, LIZ ....IT **WORKED!**

The family dynamics shifted when Grandpa moved in. At almost eight, April in many ways was "catching up" to Elizabeth. Liz resented the loss of her room and the loss of her privacy. She often resented the way Mom and Grandpa sided with the youngest child.

127

Once again, there was good stuff about being the youngest of three and there was the not-so-good stuff.

When you look through family photographs, and count the baby pictures . . . you might start to think it's better to be born first!

HOW LONG ARE YOU GOING TO STAY WITH US, GRAMPA?

PUT IT THIS WAY.... AS LONG AS I'M NEEDED.

WHAT ARE YOU DOING, APRIL?

LOOKING FOR SOMETHING TO BREAK.

Winter was long and cold. Grandpa stayed until springtime. This was when Grandma Marian's memorial service would be. The whole family was flying to Vancouver and April couldn't wait to get on the plane. She wanted to be high above the clouds, so she could watch for angels. She hoped she'd see two of them.

The memorial service was held in the park near a garden Grandma loved. Elly read a letter she had written to her mother, saying how much she'd learned from her and how much she was missed. Elizabeth sang and Uncle Phil told about her life. Marian had been a secretary and had met Jim in England, during the war. He talked about her talents, sense of humor, and he told stories about himself and Elly when they were kids. April looked at her mom . . . and wondered what she was like when she was little and how it would feel if she was gone.

Later, Michael, Elizabeth, and April went for a walk. They didn't talk as much about Grandma as they did about their own mom and dad. Michael said, "How fast time goes by."

Up until now, time hadn't really meant a lot to April (except it was a long time until Christmas and she was almost eight).

The memorial service was a good thing. It made her think about how important every hour of every day is. It made her glad her family was safe and close by, and that she hadn't bugged her sister for a whole morning! ... But, it was just a matter of time.

MICHAEL, HOWCOME A STONE CAN SKIP ACROSS THE WATER LIKE THAT?

BECAUSE IT HAS A FLAT BOTTOM

ANYTHING THAT'S SMALL AND HEAVY AND HAS A FLAT BOTTOM CAN SKIP ACROSS THE WATER.

THIS IS A GREAT BEACH!

YEAH. MOM USED TO COME HERE ALL THE TIME WHEN SHE WAS A KID.

WHY DID SHE EVER LEAVE?

SHE WENT TO UNIVERSITY IN TORONTO, GOT MARRIED—AN' THAT WAS THAT!

BESIDES, IF SHE'D STAYED HERE, SHE NEVER WOULD HAVE MET DAD, AN' IF SHE NEVER MET DAD, WE WOULDN'T BE **HERE**!

OH.

WHAT DID **DAD** HAVE TO DO WITH IT?

MICHAEL, LOOK!—I'VE GOT **CRABS**!

S'IL VOUS PLAIT

SEE? IF YOU TURN OVER ONE OF THESE ROCKS, YOU'LL FIND... **HAH!** THERE'S ANOTHER ONE!

I'VE GOT 12 OF THEM, NOW!

THAT'S COOL, APRIL. WHERE ARE YOU KEEPING THE OTHERS?

BREAD
CEREALS
PANCAKE
SYRUP
MIX
BAKING
SUPPLIES

I DON'T KNOW WHAT TO DO, JOHN... SHE'S BEEN LIKE THIS ALL AFTERNOON!

SEEMS TO ME THAT SOMEBODY NEEDS A NAP!!

Z

Every experience on the road to maturity takes you a step closer to finding out who you are. But, before you can discover yourself, you try being other people!

You copy other people's clothes, their speech, their ways of acting. You use their expressions, copy their style. You check out magazines, watch videos, play music, and study the moves of the "in crowd."

Being cool is what you're aiming for. Even semi-cool is acceptable. Anybody uncool is a nerd. You gotta fit in.

The problem with being cool and fitting in is—who makes the rules? Who decides what's cool and what isn't? Sometimes the kids making the rules are total nerds—but they look good! They're sort of like cheap gum with a great wrapper.

So you experiment around and eventually you find something that feels right. That's another big step on the road to maturity . . . and it's a big one!

Growing never stops. Questions never end. April once asked Grandma Carrie, "When do you know that you're all grown up?" Grandma answered, "I'm almost 70, and I still don't know."

April loved asking questions. The hardest to answer were the most fun to ask.

Schoolwork was getting more complicated. Duncan Anderson could spell better than anybody. April wished she was as smart as he was. "I'm not smart," he said, "I just like words."

Duncan wished he could do numbers as well as April did. "But, numbers are easy!" said April. For everyone, some stuff is easy and some stuff is hard . . . and it all seems to depend on what you like!

WHY DO I HAFTA GO TO BED WHILE 'LIZABETH'S STILL UP?

BECAUSE SHE'S DOING HOMEWORK...

AND YOU NEED YOUR SLEEP.

BUT I'M NOT TIRED! I DON'T **WANNA** GO TO BED! — I'M NOT **READY** YET !!!

GET IN. **NO!** I'M GONNA STAND HERE ALL NIGHT!

FINE.

WHY DO I HAFTA GO TO BED NOW? ELIZABETH CAN STAY UP AS LONG AS SHE WANTS TO!

APRIL, YOU'RE IN GRADE 2 AND ELIZABETH'S 18! SHE'S GROWN UP NOW, AND WE TREAT HER LIKE A GROWNUP. THERE'S A BIG DIFFERENCE BETWEEN YOU.

IF LIZ ISN'T HOME BY MIDNIGHT, WE'RE GOING TO HAVE A SERIOUS DISCUSSION.

BUT I THOUGHT YOU **WANTED** ME TO READ !!!

The more independent Elizabeth became, the more nervous April was at night. Strange things would creep into her head. She'd pull the blankets up, close her eyes, and think of good times and super heroes and sunshine.

She was used to the sounds in the hallway: footsteps, the closing of doors, and the shower running. She knew when Elizabeth was rummaging in her closet, when she got into bed, and could tell by the sound of the mattress that she'd finished a book and was turning to put out the light.

When she was small and afraid of the dark, April could crawl into bed with Elizabeth and her fears would go away.

Elizabeth could drive now and had a job downtown. April was often asleep when she came home—but just knowing that someone would be sleeping in the room across the hall was comfort enough. Sometimes.

Elly gave in and allowed April to have the dog in her room. Until now, he had slept on his bed in the hallway. She knew he'd be snuggling up to April, dirtying the blankets and shedding on the sheets. And he was good company. He'd make her feel safe.

Paw prints on a pillow meant a good night's sleep!

Grandpa's visits were something to look forward to. When he came, Elizabeth moved to Michael's room, but, like her brother, left the house to attend university. "I'm going to be a lonely child," April said to her mother. Elly laughed, "No, April—what you mean is an only child!" But, April knew what she was saying . . . and didn't want to imagine being upstairs alone.

April counted the years by Christmases. The handmade ornaments she'd brought home from kindergarten were "old" now. She started to see subtle changes in her parents. Dad's hair was going gray, and Mom complained a lot about her weight, her work—everything.

Mom said her mood swings were "menopause." Dad called it "the change of wife."

WHEN'S GRANDPA COMING TO VISIT, MOM?

NEXT WEEK! THE TIME IS GOING BY TOO FAST!!

I HAVEN'T FINISHED THE CHRISTMAS CARDS, I NEED TO SHOP, TO CLEAN...

WHEN ARE WE GONNA GET A TREE?

I DON'T KNOW, APRIL! ASK YOUR DAD ABOUT THE TREE! I CAN'T DO EVERYTHING!

IF SHE DOESN'T STOP BEING CRABBY... SANTA ISN'T GOING TO BRING HER ANYTHING!

ELIZABETH, APRIL...I'M SORRY I'VE BEEN SO SHORT-TEMPERED LATELY.

THAT'S OK. WE'RE GETTING USED TO IT.

I BOUGHT SOME MEDICATION TODAY, SO I HOPE I'LL BE FEELING BETTER SOON.

YOU'VE BEEN MOMZILLA.

I KNOW. I FEEL VERY GUILTY... AND I WANT TO MAKE IT UP TO YOU.

YOU DO?

I DON'T THINK THAT WAS THE RIGHT TIME TO ASK FOR A RAISE IN YOUR ALLOWANCE.

GRAMPA'S HERE! GRAMPA'S HERE!

*G*randpa's next visit included his new dog Dixie. "Three pets in the house!" Elly grumbled to herself as she watched two dogs and a rabbit establish their territory.

But, April was delighted. Even though he was well into his 70's, here at last was someone she could play with!

CAN'T CATCH ME, GRAMPA!

CAN'T CATCH ME!

YOU CAN'T CATCH ME! YOU CAN'T CATCH ME!!!

...GRAMPA?

GOTCHA!

GRANDPA... HOW DID JOSEPH AN' MARY AN' THE BABY STAY WARM IF IT WAS WINTER?

WELL... FOR ONE THING, THEY LIVED IN A WARM COUNTRY.

LET'S GET THE ATLAS!

HERE'S ISRAEL. IT'S ON THE MEDITERRANEAN SEA BETWEEN LEBANON AND EGYPT!

COOL! GRANDPA... WHY IS THIS BOOK CALLED AN ATLAS?

BECAUSE WHEN YOU DON'T KNOW WHERE A COUNTRY IS, AND YOU LOOK IT UP IN HERE, YOU CAN SAY, "LOOK! ATLAS I'VE FOUND IT!"

WORLD ATLAS

WHY ARE YOU SO SILLY, GRANDPA?

IT KEEPS ME YOUNG.

SEE? THE LITTLE HAND IS ON 5 AN' THE BIG HAND IS ON 12. THAT MEANS IT'S 5 O'CLOCK.

WHERE IS EVERYBODY?

DON'T THEY KNOW IT'S **CHRISTMAS?!**

NOW I LAY ME DOWN TO SLEEP- A BAG OF PEANUTS AT MY FEET, IF I SHOULD DIE BEFORE I WAKE, I'LL EAT THEM AT ST. PETER'S GATE.

WHO TAUGHT YOU THAT?

GRAMPA!

WELL, IT'S NOT A REAL PRAYER, APRIL, A PRAYER IS WHEN YOU ASK GOD TO BLESS SOMEONE OR TO FORGIVE YOU. MAYBE YOU WANT TO ASK FOR SOMETHING...OR JUST SAY 'THANK YOU.'

OH...

THEN IS IT OK IF I EAT THEM NOW?

WELL, DID YOU HAVE A GOOD TIME SKIING?

GREAT!

YAH!

WHAT HAPPENED?

I TOOK DOWN THE TREE AND PUT AWAY ALL THE CHRISTMAS DECORATIONS.

YOU MEAN, IT'S OVER?

UH HUH! EVERYONE'S BACK IN SCHOOL TO-MORROW -AND WE'RE INTO A BRAND-NEW YEAR.

WE ARE?!

TSK ... NOBODY TELLS ME **ANYFING!**

143

FOR BETTER OR FOR WORSE

By Lynn Johnston

KNEAD PUSH... PAT SPRINKLE -ROLL ROLL

MOM... I'M BORED. I'VE GOT NOTHIN' TO DO.

MOM, CAN I GO TO BECKY'S?

NO, HONEY. IT'S TOO CLOSE TO SUPPERTIME.

BUT, I WANNA GO TO BECKY'S!

NOT TONIGHT.

AAAUGH! IT'S NO FAIR!

APRIL, THAT'S NO WAY TO BEHAVE.

FIRST OF ALL, YOU NEED MORE ANGST IN YOUR VOICE. AND TRY SOME FLOOR POUNDING.

LIKE THIS! **AAG!** WHY CAN'T I GO?!! AAAAAHH

THEN, YOU COULD ROLL OVER. AAAAUUGHH!!

DADDY, CUT IT OUT.

WHAT?

I SAID STOP IT. YOU'RE BEING STUPID.

...OH.

APRIL'S QUIET. DID YOU HAVE A TALK WITH HER?

UH HUH.

GOOD! IT'S ABOUT TIME SHE LEARNED HOW TO HANDLE THINGS WITH A LITTLE MORE MATURITY.

Panel 1: WHAT DID MOM WANT TO TALK TO YOU PRIVATELY ABOUT, LIZ? / SHE KNOWS I WENT INTO A BAR THE OTHER NIGHT, AN' SHE'S NOT TOO HAPPY ABOUT IT.

Panel 2: YOU **DID?!!**- THAT'S COOL! — WHAT WAS IT LIKE?

Panel 3: WELL, IT WAS SMOKY AND DIRTY AN' A CREEPY OLD GUY TRIED TO PICK UP ONE OF MY FRIENDS. IT WAS PRETTY BORING, ACTUALLY. / YEAH.

Panel 4: ...THAT'S THE TROUBLE WITH A LOT OF STUFF YOU'RE NOT SUPPOSED TO DO!

April looked like a kid, played like a kid and still threw the occasional tantrum. But by the age of eight, things were happening. Things her parents didn't see.

April knew about the other side, the darker side of life. It wasn't enough to be told you shouldn't do something, it was time to find out "why." She took coins from a bowl on her father's dresser. She stole gum from the corner store and the rush of getting away with it felt . . . weird. She threw bottles on the rocks, just to see them shatter, then lied to her teacher at school. Some of her friends used curse words. They kicked and punched like guys in the movies. One of them knew where to get real beer.

There was a kid who lived in a house on 6th Street, whose parents were never home. Together, they looked at bad sites on the internet and played some of the games. He gave them cigarettes and matches. They tried smoking. Coughing and with teary eyes, they pretended it was good. Being with the kids on 6th Street felt exciting and dangerous. It was cool to be wild and irresponsible, but the feelings followed her and turned to guilt when she got home.

April told only Becky about the things she'd done. They told each other everything. They had other secrets, too. They wore Becky's mom's make-up and her jewelry. They looked through all her private dresser drawers. They even got undressed together and compared bodies to see who was changing faster.

There were changes everywhere: mental, social, physical. It was a time to experiment.

Life is a buffet of good and bad, right and wrong and at the age of eight, you want to taste it all.

145

She was learning a lot about herself. She'd done things she was sorry for, but she wouldn't do them again. April knew, deep down, she was OK.

When she collected money for school it would have been easy to keep some—but it was more fun to turn over the whole amount. Feeling proud was awesome. It felt better than stealing, better than lying, better than "hoping you don't get caught."

She had tried some bad stuff . . . and good was definitely better.

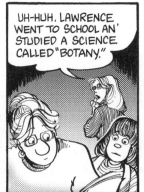

AND, DON'T FORGET TO BRING ME THE CHANGE!

*H*er youngest daughter could be trusted. Elly was sure of that. April had permission to use the computer and to watch TV with her friends unsupervised. The kids preferred good shows to garbage and Elly knew they'd seen enough to know the difference.

Becky and Duncan were often at the Patterson house, especially on weekends. Duncan would come with his father who liked model railroads and spent many hours with John. Becky came by on her bicycle or was dropped off by her mother. She liked being at April's house. There was always something going on.

April was glad her mom liked having kids in the house. Some moms didn't. Having kids in the house meant more noise, more interruptions, more mess to clean up. But, Elly saw it as an opportunity. Getting to know the people April played with told her a lot about her daughter. It also meant that most of the time—she knew where she was!

BECKY, IF YOU'RE GONNA HAVE THE CLICKER, STAY ON ONE CHANNEL FOR A WHILE!

CLICK CLIK CLICK CLICK CLIK

NOT THAT ONE, IT'S MOSTLY SEX AGAIN. FIND SOMETHING WITHOUT THE BORING SCORING.

CLICK CLICK

MORE VIAGRA JOKES, MORE BORING SCORING, BORING SCORING... MAN! WHY ARE SO MANY OF THESE SHOWS SO UGLY AN' STUPID AN' DUMB?

CLICK CLICK

THEY'RE FOR GROWN-UPS.

MOM, EDGAR GOT INTO THE POPCORN AND...

APRIL, I'M TRYING TO WORK!

I AM LEARNING HOW TO USE THE WORD PROCESSOR AND I AM NOT HAVING A WONDERFUL TIME, OK? AND EVERY TIME YOU INTERRUPT ME, I GET VERY FRUSTRATED.

SO, YOU CAN EITHER HANDLE THE PROBLEM YOURSELVES OR YOU CAN STAY HERE AND WATCH ME TURN INTO A DROOLING, SCREAMING, RAVING, FIRE-BELCHING LUNATIC!

MOM, BECKY AN' DUNCAN AND I ARE PRETTY GOOD AT THE COMPUTER. CAN WE SHOW YOU?

NO.

AAAUGH! I HATE THIS MACHINE!!!

NO, LEAVE HER ALONE, APRIL.

THEY NEVER LEARN IF YOU DON'T LET THEM FIGURE THINGS OUT FOR THEMSELVES.

SNIFF? SNOOF? SNUFFA SNIFFA SNIFF SNUFF

SNURREFAH SNIFF SNIFFA SNUFF SNUFF SNF SNF FF FF F SNUFFFFF!

SNIFF? SNOOOF! SSSSS SNIFF SNUF SNIF? SNF

CHOMP!

APRIL, NEXT TIME YOU EAT BUTTERED POPCORN... DON'T WIPE YOUR HANDS ON THE RABBIT!

She was almost nine. She'd grown out of her favorite overalls and her shoes were a ladies size 5. She measured herself back to back with Elizabeth. "Now I'm really catching up," she said.

She'd lost interest in her turtles and goldfish—and Elly had put away many toys. Things like blading and bicycles took their place. She asked for a snowboard for Christmas.

When she played sports, she was serious. When she skated, she had to compete. Evenings were spent at the gym and arena.

Elly and John took turns driving her from one event to another, wanting her to experience everything, even if it meant no time for themselves.

Tuesday was bowling, Wednesday was dance, Thursday she skated, and in between were school events and other things.

April overheard Elly complaining to John: "April is involved in too many things,' she said. "But, she wants to do them," he argued. It was a discussion they'd had before.

Sometimes Elizabeth would take her to a game or a lesson, but she resented "babysitting" when she had to do it too often. "Babysitting." April hated the word.

The family got together. They said it was up to April to decide what to continue with and what to let go. She wanted to do everything! As long as her marks were OK, they'd encouraged her to do whatever held her interest, and now she was criticized for doing too much.

It wasn't fair.

I'M SORRY, LIZ. THAT'S OK. I SHOULD HAVE CALLED AND SAID I WASN'T COMING HOME FOR SUPPER.

IT'S JUST THAT, WHEN I **AM** HOME, YOU EXPECT ME TO WATCH OVER APRIL ALL THE TIME... AND MAYBE I'VE GOT OTHER STUFF TO DO.

AND, DON'T FORGET, I'LL BE LEAVING FOR UNIVERSITY IN THE FALL. YOU'LL HAVE TO FIND A BABY SITTER AGAIN!

YOU'RE RIGHT. THAT'S A PROBLEM.

DID YOU HEAR THAT, EDDY? ... I'M A PROBLEM!

There was tension in the air. Even if nothing was said, you could feel it.

Elizabeth was pulling away from the family, separating herself from home.

Mom and Dad were acting differently. There was a problem, and April thought it was her.

HEY, SHORTSTUFF... WHAT'S WRONG?

I HEARD YOU TALKING. NOBODY WANTS ME AROUND.

APRIL, THAT'S NOT TRUE. WE WERE JUST SAYING THAT WHEN I GO AWAY TO UNIVERSITY, IT WILL BE DIFFERENT. THAT'S ALL.

MAYBE MOM AND DAD WILL HAVE TO HIRE A SITTER SOMETIMES, AND...

I DON'T WANT A SITTER! IF I HAFTA HAVE SOME UGLY, DUMB PERSON WATCHING ME AT NIGHT...

I WANT IT TO BE **YOU!!**

FOR Better OR FOR WORSE®

By Lynn Johnston

SNIFF?

ELIZABETH, I WANT YOU TO TELL ME SOMETHING ABOUT THESE.

EASTER EGGS!

WELL, IT'S A REALLY OLD TRADITION, APRIL. AN EGG SIGNIFIES BIRTH—AND THIS IS THE BIRTH OF SPRING!

THE WORD "EASTER" COMES FROM THE NAME "EASTRE" WHO WAS ONCE BELIEVED TO BE THE GODDESS OF SPRING!

OF COURSE, EASTER IS A VERY IMPORTANT RELIGIOUS CELEBRATION WHICH MIGHT SEEM LIKE A CELEBRATION ABOUT DEATH...

BUT, ACCORDING TO THE BIBLE, JESUS DIED AND CAME TO LIFE AGAIN— JUST LIKE ALL THE LEAVES AND FLOWERS AND ANIMALS COME BACK IN SPRINGTIME!

SO, THAT'S WHY WE HAVE EGGS WHEN WE CELEBRATE EASTER!

DOES THAT ANSWER YOUR QUESTION, APRIL?

NOT REALLY

I WANTED TO KNOW WHO ATE ALL THE CHOCOLATE ONES!!

151

If a kid thinks she's a problem, but isn't quite sure, she becomes a problem! Then, everything makes sense.

Even though she loved Elizabeth, April did what she could do to provoke her—then everyone was angry!

This was OK. It was better than tension. It was better than not knowing what was wrong at all.

Michael was graduating from university. It was an exciting day. The family prepared for the three-hour drive to London and for the most part, they rode in silence.

"I'm sorry," April said finally. "For what?" said Elly. "Everybody's mad at me, so I thought I'd say I was sorry." "But you haven't done anything," said John. "Then," sighed April, "why is everyone so grouchy?"

Elly and John didn't know they'd been acting differently. All they knew was Michael was now a free man and this would be their last year with Elizabeth. They were happy, they were sad, they were optimistic, they were scared—they were full of mixed emotions. That's what all the tension was about. They laughed and told April that nothing was her fault.

Strange how tension disappears when you talk about it.

FOR Better OR FOR WORSE

By Lynn Johnston

HONEY, HAVE YOU SEEN MY GARDENING GLOVES?

I THINK I HUNG THEM UP IN THE GARAGE.

KNOW WHAT I SAW ON TV, MOM?

THIS GUY HUNG SOME GLOVES ON A NAIL LIKE THAT AN' A SPIDER WENT INSIDE ONE OF THE FINGERS.

THEN, WHEN HE PUT HIS GLOVES ON — IT BIT HIM, LIKE **THIS!**

HIS FINGER SWELLED UP SO MUCH, HE HAD TO GO TO THE HOSPITAL!

DID YOUR MOM FIND HER GARDENING GLOVES, APRIL?

UH HUH

AN' SHE'S JUMPING UP AN' DOWN ON THEM!

Lynn

When real life got too complicated, April could still escape into fantasy. She could travel to different worlds—all of her own invention. In one, she had super powers, in another she went to the future, imagining herself owning horses, growing her hair down to her knees, having children of her own. She could also go back to the past. It was wonderful, like dreaming with your eyes open.

She was allowed to go to the river alone now. Farley's tree was a short walk down the ravine. If she was in a thinking mood, her family knew they could find her there. She could sit under the tree and imagine. She could fly to somewhere else, faraway—and the best part was . . . Farley went with her.

Out of sight, but never out of mind, she was given freedom to explore. When it came to choices, Elly and John hoped she would make the right ones.

April was entering the passageway that lead to adulthood, even though she still looked like a child. Like a rider on a runaway steed, her thoughts raced ahead of her developing body.

CAN'T CATCH ME! CAN'T CATCH ME!

SHRIEK! HA HA

THAT'S ENOUGH, APRIL I CAN'T PLAY ANY MORE. I'M EXHAUSTED!

ELIZABETH... YOU'RE NOT GETTING OLD, ARE YOU?

WHATCHA DOIN', ELIZABETH?

GOING THROUGH ALL MY STUFF SO I KNOW WHAT TO PACK!

I'VE GOTTA DECIDE WHICH CLOTHES TO TAKE AN' OTHER THINGS, LIKE MY SKIS, MY CDS, MY CLOCK, LAMP, SEWING KIT...

ARE YOU GONNA TAKE YOUR OLD CLOTH BUNNY?

SURE! I HAVE TO TAKE MY CLOTH BUNNY!

THEN YOU REALLY ARE LEAVING, AREN'T YOU?

APRIL, WHAT'S THE MATTER?

ELIZABETH IS PACKING AND SHE'S GOING TO GO AWAY.

I KNOW. SHE'LL BE IN A NEW SCHOOL IN A NEW TOWN— BUT WE'LL VISIT AND WE'LL SEE HER ON HOLIDAYS AND WE'LL WRITE!

I DON'T WANT HER TO GO!!

PEOPLE GROW UP, HONEY, AND THEY START LIVES OF THEIR OWN! SOME DAY YOU'LL GO AWAY, TOO.

THEN I'LL TRY AN' GROW UP AS SLOWLY AS POSSIBLE.

In the twilight zone between child and teen-ager, April desperately needed all of the things she was pushing away.

She needed the guidance of her parents, even though rules and curfews infuriated her. She needed the consistency of schedules, even though she wanted to make up her own. She needed help with things she wanted to do by herself and when she pushed away the people she loved, that's when she needed their hugs and understanding most of all.

April needed Elizabeth. Their lives had been spinning off in different directions, but she needed her just the same. Just the words, "Big Sister," were comforting. A big sister isn't always an authority figure. She's someone with whom you can argue, say what you feel, shout at, fight, make up with—and come to when you're scared . . . (but don't want sympathy from Mom or Dad).

Everyone was excited for Elizabeth when she left home for university. April watched her pack, taking with her familiar personal things: her pictures, tennis racquet, favorite clothes, hiking boots, and party clothes.

The stuffed rabbit that had always been on Liz's dresser was the last to go into her knapsack. Tucked lovingly into the top, the worn old bunny was leaving too, a piece of Elizabeth's own childhood was leaving the house she'd grown up in.

Saying goodbye to her sister was, for a while, more than April could bear. She tried to keep the feelings inside. She thought she'd rather fall off her bicycle and break something. Perhaps the pain would be easier to take and faster to heal.

For Better or For Worse®
By Lynn Johnston

MOM? UHHH?

I'M SCARED. I DON'T WANNA SLEEP UPSTAIRS BY MYSELF. I MISS ELIZABETH!

HONEY, ELIZABETH IS IN UNIVERSITY NOW.

I WANT YOU AN' DADDY TO MOVE UPSTAIRS AGAIN. I DON'T **WANNA** BE ALONE!

WHY DON'T YOU GO BACK TO BED, AND I'LL COME AND SLEEP IN ELIZABETH'S ROOM TONIGHT.

SNIFF.. OK.

ELLY, WE TALKED ABOUT THIS! APRIL HAS THE DOG IN HER ROOM, SHE HAS HER RADIO, HER TOYS. SHE SAID SHE'D BE FINE!

SHE EVEN SAID SHE WANTED TO BE ALONE-THAT IT WOULD MAKE HER FEEL ALL GROWN UP!

I KNOW.

THESE THINGS ALWAYS WORK WELL IN THEORY.

It took courage to sleep on the upper floor all by herself. The sounds of the night became commonplace and the bonds between herself and her parents were closer now.

April became more aware of the things she had in common with her dad. She let him teach her now. She found herself listening.

School and friends became her second family. Her day didn't begin until Becky and Duncan were there. She fit in with these people like a puzzle piece. They were part of her—and in them she could see the mirror of her own progress and development.

April had a love for her schoolmates that transcended friendship. It was something a kid can't describe.

Rebellion isn't something you plan, it just happens. One day, the command to "clean up your room" is as irksome as a gnat up your nose. The next day . . . it detonates an explosion.

The need to test authority is sort of like one's need to test pain. Pain is important, you need it, you don't like it . . . but you always want to know it's still there.

PEPPERONI STICK, CHEESE 'N' CRACKERS, JUICE BOX, GRANOLA BAR!

LOOK, MOM—I MADE MY OWN LUNCH!

GOOD FOR YOU! CAN I SEE?

HOW ABOUT ADDING AN APPLE OR AN ORANGE... AND SOME CARROT STICKS?

I LIKE TO KNOW YOU HAVE SOME HEALTHY NATURAL FOODS IN THERE!

...I ALSO LIKE TO BELIEVE THAT YOU EAT THEM.

Cc Dd Ee Ff Gg

Dd Ee Ff Gg

OK, APRIL AND GERALD... YOU CAN EACH DO FOUR EXTRA MATH PROBLEMS AT HOME TONIGHT.

HOW DO THEY KNOW?

I DUNNO... THEY JUST DO.

HOW WAS SCHOOL TODAY, APRIL?

OK—EXCEPT FOR ENGLISH. WE HAD TO DRAW CIRCLES AN' LOOPS, CIRCLES AN' LOOPS...

FOR HOMEWORK, WE HAFTA MAKE ROWS AN' ROWS OF ALPHABET LETTERS.

THEN WHEN WE KNOW HOW TO DO THEM RIGHT, WE'RE SUPPOSED TO JOIN THEM TOGETHER.

THAT'S CALLED "CURSIVE" WRITING!

REALLY?!

*@☆Ø

166

Another December. Grandpa Jim was, like April, getting used to living on his own. Having a dog helped—and spending Christmas with his daughter was something he looked forward to. It was like coming home. April was almost nine now. She welcomed visitors upstairs as if she owned that part of the house—for, in her mind, it was hers!

April was used to her space alone. Two empty bedrooms on the same floor weren't as spooky as they'd once been. Still the fun of having Elizabeth and Grandpa there filled the upstairs with noise and laughter; sounds she had missed so much. She wanted to hear those sounds every morning. Not just on holidays.

Moving Grandpa Jim, kit and caboodle, into the Patterson house wasn't a simple thing. First of all, they had to convince him to do so. Could he leave his home in Vancouver? Could he pull away from the memories and from the cemetery where he went to visit Marian almost every week?

It meant Elly and John would vacate a room they'd just added to the house, but for Grandpa the room was perfect! It was private, with a bathroom, and enough space for his desk and other personal treasures.

With April's arms around his neck and Elly's reassurances, Jim Richards agreed to move east. Elly and John returned to their old bedroom and once again, April had company—both upstairs and down! Even the pets were happy.

We all talk about "family dynamics." The fact that the words dynamics and dynamite sound similar may not be just a coincidence.

Inviting someone to live with you is a generous and well-intended gesture but it throws another flavor into the "people pudding" that already exists.

A family runs like a wheel. Each spoke supports the rim on which the family unit moves. Alter or remove a spoke and the wheel runs differently.

Grandpa was an extra spoke—and often, quite outspoken. Even though Elly was almost fifty, she was still his child. He gave "helpful criticism," told anecdotes she'd heard ad nauseam, slurped his tea—and sided with April who used her new ally like a Star Wars shield: silent, invisible, and easily deployed. The wheel wobbled. Elly and John could have managed easily were it nor for the big change she was facing herself. Menopause was no longer a mild discomfort. At the slightest provocation, it was setting Elly off like a spark in methane, and she didn't know how to control

it. Her hot flashes, cold sweats, sleeplessness, and depression made life difficult for everyone. John began to wonder if the girl he married had been replaced by an unpredictable clone.

Grandpa had seen "the change." It took Elly's mother years to go through it. He knew what was happening, but that didn't make it any easier.

A new dynamic began to form: April, Grandpa, and John . . . against Mom.

Jim Richards kept to himself a little more. Going through his things, he found the harmonica he'd bought during the war. It still worked, and the old tunes brought back such memories!

"Please teach me how to play," begged April. With time and patience, Jim taught her and soon she could play simple melodies. "You're someone who knows how to carry a tune !" he said to her—and he gave her the treasured instrument to keep.

April had been in fights before, but not like the one with Jeremy Jones. For some reason, the sound of the harmonica ignited a hatred in him and he declared all-out war.

She retaliated by making up songs about him, which made things worse. There was excitement in provoking a boy like Jeremy, but there was danger too.

176

When Jeremy saw April alone on her bicycle, he went after her. He wanted to hurt her. In his rage, he swerved into the path of an oncoming car and was seriously injured.

April faced a real test now. Should she help him or turn and run? It would have been easier to run, but fear turned to compassion. She called and waited for help. The whole ordeal had been awful. The hardest part, however, was going with her mother to see the boy who had tried so hard to run her down— the boy who had so much anger inside. In the hospital, she found a different Jeremy. Gone was the defiance. Gone was the cruelty. This Jeremy could cry.

He was surprised to see her. It made no sense. An act of kindness! From now on, it would be hard for him to hate her. It would be hard to know what to think.

What makes people enemies is a complex mixture of things, but mostly it's not knowing or understanding someone else. It's hard to care about someone you don't know or understand.

Although April and Jeremy will never be friends, he treats her differently now. He can't quite explain what happened and he can't quite explain what he feels. But perhaps there's a word that defines the truce between them. Perhaps the word is "respect."

I CALLED THE HOSPITAL. THEY'RE NOT TELLING ME MUCH BECAUSE WE'RE NOT FAMILY, BUT THEY DO SAY HE'S GOING TO BE FINE.

THE AMBULANCE PEOPLE GAVE ME JEREMY'S HELMET TO LOOK AFTER. EVERYBODY ACTED LIKE I WAS HIS **FRIEND!**

WELL, YOU CALLED FOR HELP, YOU STAYED BY HIS SIDE, YOU CARED ABOUT HIM WHEN HE WAS HURT.

BUT, WHO WOULDN'T?!!

THE SAD ANSWER TO THAT QUESTION, APRIL, IS—LOTS OF PEOPLE.

GOING TO VISIT JEREMY IN THE HOSPITAL FEELS WEIRD, MOM.

BUT I THINK IT'S THE RIGHT THING TO DO.

ROOM 217... HIS MOTHER IS WITH HIM.

THANKS.

MRS. JONES?-I'M ELLY PATTERSON AND THIS IS MY DAUGHTER, APRIL.

JEREMY, HONEY? SOMEONE'S HERE TO SEE YOU.

HE'S CRYING. IS HE ALL RIGHT?

YEAH... IT'S PROBABLY BECAUSE YOU'RE THE ONLY FRIEND WHO'S COME TO VISIT HIM SO FAR!

WELL, I GUESS WE SHOULD GO, YOUR HUSBAND AND FAMILY WILL BE HERE SOON.

NAH... IT'S JUST ME AND JEREMY.

HIS DAD DON'T LIVE WITH US. HE HIT THE ROAD WHEN JER. WAS REAL SMALL. HE'S A MUSICIAN... PROBABLY OUT WEST RIGHT NOW.

REALLY!

WHAT DOES HE PLAY?

OH... SOME GUITAR, A LITTLE DRUMS, SOME KEYBOARD...

BUT, MOSTLY, HE PLAYS THE HARMONICA.

FOR BETTER OR FOR WORSE By Lynn Johnston

GRIND GRIND GRIND GRIND GRIND GRIND GRIND

GRIND GRIND GRIND

WHHHH

CRUNCH CRUNCH CHEW CRUNK CRUNCH CHEW CHEW CRUNCH CRUNCH CHEW CRUNCH CHEW

CRUNCH CHEW CRUNCH CRUNCH CHEW CRUNCH

PSSTT...HEY, APRIL, COULD I BORROW ONE OF YER PENCILS?

SURE!

UHHMMM.... MAYBE I'LL ASK DUNCAN IF I CAN BORROW ONE OF HIS.

OK

MAN, THIS IS SO COOL.

LAST YEAR, I TRIED TO HANG ONTO MY PENCILS BY PUTTING MY **NAME** ON THEM!!

Young parents toss their kids in the air, give them horseback rides, match them at tennis, and race them to the corner and back.

As April began to start "feeling her oats," Elly and John started feeling their age. Elly began hormone replacement therapy and John thought he needed to replace everything.

OH, WOW! A PORCUPINE!

DAD! GRAMPA, LOOK! THERE'S A PORCUPINE UP IN THAT TREE!

WHERE? I DON'T SEE HIM.

NEITHER DO I.

HE'S RIGHT THERE!!

IT MUST BE AN OLD NEST, APRIL.

OR A BUNCH OF DRIED LEAVES.

BUT IT'S A PORCUPINE! HONEST!!

WAIT A MINUTE - I SEE HIM!

YOU DO?!!

SEE? HE'S AT THE VERY TOP OF THAT TALL BIRCH OVER THERE!

SORRY - I DON'T SEE ANYTHING.

WELL! I GUESS YOU WERE RIGHT, HONEY!

DADDY...

HOW COME GROWN-UPS BELIEVE OTHER GROWN-UPS... BUT THEY DON'T BELIEVE ME?

WHERE'S MOM AN' DAD?

THEY'RE MEETING WITH MRS. PETRUCCI.

ARE THEY GONNA BUY HER STORE?

I DON'T KNOW

I HOPE THEY DO!

WELL, DON'T HOLD YOUR BREATH. THEY'D NEVER MAKE A DECISION LIKE THAT IN ONE EVENING.

&lly's decision to buy a little book-and-toy shop came as a surprise to everyone. She'd never seen herself as a businesswoman, but here was an opportunity she couldn't resist. It was a decision that involved everyone.

There were many changes to be made, but they voted to keep the name. Lilliput's, it just sounded right. Suddenly, they were infused with energy! This was good. Elizabeth's summer at home now included working at the store—cataloging, moving, setting things aside for sale. Michael came home and helped his dad remove shelves, boxes, and file cabinets

ALL THIS STUFF IS OURS?

YES. WE'LL HAVE TO CLEAN OUT THIS WHOLE SPACE AND DO A MASSIVE INVENTORY.

WE?

GAMES

MONOPOLY

STUFFED TOYS

that had been in the shop basement for years. A cache of very old toys was discovered, and the windfall helped pay for renovations to the roof, ceiling, and floors. When the paint dried, John put a big train display in the window and Grandpa said it was the most welcoming store on the block.

April couldn't believe that her mom owned a real book-and-toy store! It was Christmas, it was heaven, it was wall-to-wall stuff!

The euphoria lasted until inventory—which was supposed to take one day, but took three. The "riches" became merchandise, product, and stock.

April dusted, sorted, counted, and cleaned. There were a couple of cool aspects to the whole affair: April earned a salary and she could keep anything too soiled or broken to sell. She took home torn teddies, stained Santas, a giraffe with a bent neck, battered books, and a jack-in-the-box with a broken spring. Some things she embraced as if they'd asked to be rescued. Most she planned to give away, but not until they'd been carefully and lovingly repaired.

April loved the toy store. She spent weekends and evenings there with her mother, helping to make it a go. It wasn't all fun. It was hard work. There was so much to do; so much to learn—but it was new and challenging. Best of all, she had Elly all to herself. They'd always be mother and daughter, but now they were friends.

For BETTER or for WORSE

By Lynn Johnston

APRIL!

APRIL, I THOUGHT I ASKED YOU TO PUT THE SPRINKLER OUT ON THE LAWN!

WHY DO I HAFTA DO IT? WHY DON'TCHA ASK ELIZABETH ?!!

BECAUSE, WATERING THE GARDEN IS **YOUR** JOB!

SSSSTTTTTT SSSSTTTTTTT SSSSTTTTT SSTTTTTT SSTT SSSTTT SSSTTT SSSTTT TTT

Lynn

There's no doubt the store took its toll on the family. Financially and emotionally, it was a strain, but it gave April and Elizabeth some equality, despite their age difference. Michael regarded it all as an adventure worth writing about, which he did!

They added hobby supplies to their expanding list of goods, and John became more interested in modeling than ever before. Together with friends from the rail club, he created a more elaborate window with so much to see that people came back time and again to make sure they hadn't missed anything!

John was so inspired by his window that he decided to build an outdoor model railroad. Grandpa Jim and April helped. Most evenings and every weekend, Elly could watch them working, right up until Halloween.

DON'T YOU THINK WE SHOULD HAVE BROUGHT YOUR MINIATURE VILLAGE INSIDE TONIGHT, JOHN?

NAH.....

IT'S SUCH A NICE LITTLE THING. I DON'T THINK ANYONE WILL TOUCH IT.

MOM? DAD? COME QUICK! I HEAR SOMETHING — IT'S IN THE FRONT YARD! HURRY!

BOWOWOWF! BARK BARK BOWF OW OW!

ISN'T IT AMAZING HOW THINGS THAT TAKE AGES TO BUILD ARE DESTROYED SO QUICKLY.

THIS LITTLE HOUSE CAN BE REPAIRED, JOHN.

I THINK I CAN SALVAGE THE STATION.

THAT WAS SUCH A NICE LITTLE VILLAGE. WHY WOULD ANYONE WANT TO WRECK IT?

I DON'T KNOW...

THERE ARE PEOPLE OUT THERE WHO JUST ENJOY BREAKING THINGS, APRIL. I GUESS IT GIVES THEM A SENSE OF POWER.

I THINK IT GIVES THEM ..... NO SENSE AT ALL.

The destruction of John's model railway hurt and disappointed everyone. All they could do was ask "Why?" April was too angry to cry. John said it took too much energy to hate people and resolved to build a better railway when he had the time. April was surprised by his acceptance.

She was also surprised by Jeremy Jones. He owed her something and now, in his own way, he was able to give back.

April had grown up in a protective, loving environment. She had experimented just so far with "the other side," but she had no idea what was out there. Images on television and newspaper headlines were about things that happened to other people.

It was Grandpa who told her about the power of pride and the glory of honor. He talked about cruelty and justice and that compromise was the solution to everything. "Nothing worthwhile was ever accomplished without compromise," he said.

*A*long with his wisdom, Grandpa Jim gave April the gift of music. He said that music was as natural as a heartbeat and as important as the food we eat. It's a journey, an expression, a message, and a cry. Music speaks for you and to you and about you.

He bought April a guitar and told her to hold it as if it were an extension of her body, as if it were part of her. In time, she learned that what he'd said was true. She found where music comes from—somewhere deep within.

VERY GOOD, APRIL. YOUR NOTES ARE CLEAR, AND YOUR TIMING IS BETTER.

LET'S TRY THIS PIECE NOW—WITH THE METRO-NOME.

I HATE THE METRO-NOME!

WHY CAN'T I JUST PLAY IT THE WAY I **WANT** TO?

THIS KID PUTS THE WORD "IMP" INTO "IMPROVISE"!

KNOW WHAT HAPPENS AFTER MY GUITAR LESSON, MR. BERGAN?—I HEAR THE MUSIC OVER AND OVER IN MY HEAD!

THEN, I CAN'T WAIT TO GO HOME AN' PRACTICE—'CAUSE I WANT TO HEAR IT AGAIN FOR REAL!!

OH,... MY DAD GAVE ME A CHEQUE FOR YOU.

THANK YOU.

... SOMETIMES, YOU FEEL YOU'VE ALREADY BEEN PAID!

THAT WAS FUN, GRAMPA!

I'LL SHOW YOU SOME MORE TUNES LATER, OK?

DAD, I DON'T THINK IT'S A GOOD IDEA.... YOU KNOW, TEACHING APRIL HOW TO PLAY BY EAR.

BUT, ELLY, IF YOU LEARN BY READING ALONE AND YOU DON'T HAVE THE SHEET MUSIC, YOU CAN'T PLAY AT ALL!!

MUSIC IS A NATURAL THING! INSTRUMENTS CAME BEFORE PAPER!

I DON'T CARE!

—I JUST WANT HER TO LEARN THE CORRECT WAY, FIRST.

THERE **ISN'T** ONE!!!

You've been smoking again, haven't you, Dad?" Elly said as a whiff of tobacco entered the house with him.

"Just a little," he admitted, taking the crushed butt from his pocket and putting it in the trash.

"You said you were quitting. You promised."

"I only smoke when I have to!" he countered. "It's only when I need a lift."

"You'll get a lift!" said his daughter. "And it's going to be in an ambulance!"

Ever since her mom died, Elly watched her dad's battle with nicotine, hoping he'd triumph over a habit he'd enjoyed since he was 17.

John often walked with his father-in-law along the lane behind the house. On one of their walks, Grandpa felt his chest, lost his footing, and fell.

An ambulance was called and he was admitted to the hospital for surgery. "Grandpa," whispered April, "can you hear me?" Jim opened his eyes and looked at his granddaughter. "I want to play something on my guitar," she said, and flawlessly played a piece he had taught her. "I wanted to give you a present," she told him, but it was more than a gift. It was a wake-up call.

ALCOHOL IS BEING BLAMED FOR A SERIOUS ACCIDENT ON THE SHEA VALLEY PARKWAY...

SEVERAL YOUTHS ARE BEING HELD RESPONSIBLE FOR A VIOLENT ROBBERY THIS AFTERNOON....

FLOOD VICTIMS CLAIM THAT FOOD, SUPPLIES AND MEDICATION INTENDED FOR THEM WAS DIVERTED AND SOLD ON THE BLACK MARKET....

ANOTHER ATTACK LEAVES SOLDIERS DEAD AND WOUNDED....

CARELESS SMOKING RESULTED IN A FIRE EARLY THIS MORNING LEAVING SIX PEOPLE HOMELESS....

TWO PEOPLE HAVE BEEN CHARGED WITH CRUELTY TO ANIMALS AFTER NEIGHBORS COMPLAINED...

GRAMPA, IS THERE EVER A DAY ON EARTH WHEN SOMETHING SAD DOESN'T HAPPEN?

—I DON'T THINK SO, APRIL!

SOME DAY... I WANT TO VISIT ANOTHER PLANET.

$\mathcal{N}$ow, April was 10! At least, she was one day away from it. Ten was what she'd been waiting for. "I'm two digits!" she shouted to her sister on the phone. "I'MGOING TO BE 10!" she e-mailed to her brother—all in capital letters.

It wasn't the longed-for "teen," but it was close enough. Half of 20. Two times five. Ten was awesome! April had gone from diapers to denims, from shy to sure (sort of), and from now on her freedoms would multiply.

She had experienced hate and hurt, guilt and envy. She knew there was a good side to life and a side they call "evil." She believed in God and family and love and friendship. She also believed in herself. April could look in the mirror now and see a glimpse of the woman she was going to become.

April's now a young girl with experience, abilities, and understanding of what's expected of her

Growing up all too fast—almost 10!

IT'S ONE O'CLOCK IN THE MORNING! -WHY DO THEY CALL THIS A **SLEEP** OVER?

BECAUSE, WE GET TO SLEEP WHEN IT'S OVER !!

ELLY, YOU JUST HAD A BIG BIRTHDAY PARTY FOR YOUR DAD— ARE YOU SURE YOU DON'T MIND ANOTHER PARTY IN THE HOUSE?

APRIL REALLY WANTS A SLEEPOVER, JOHN.

BUT 7 KIDS!

IT'LL KEEP US AWAKE UNTIL MIDNIGHT!

THAT'S OK .... SOME DAY, SHE'LL BE KEEPING US AWAKE UNTIL MIDNIGHT ....

.... AND, WE WON'T KNOW WHERE SHE IS.

YOU LIKE GERALD, DON'T YOU, APRIL.

OH, AS IF !!!

WE KNOW YOU DO! IT IS SOOO OBVIOUS!

WELL, BECKY LIKES MARK, AN' CHANTAL LIKES BRENDAN!

OH YAH?

DID YOU EVER KISS ANY-ONE?

NOPE!

I DID!

REALLY? WHAT WAS IT LIKE?!!

FIRST OF ALL, YOU GOTTA FIGURE OUT WHERE TO PUT YOUR NOSE!

CHANTAL LOVES BRENDAN!

SHUT UP!

KISSY KISSY

I WISH I HADN'T TOLD YOU GUYS, IT WAS 'NO BIG DEAL...., HIS LIPS FELT LIKE FUZZ.

SHREIK!!
GIGGLE GIGGLE
HOWLLLLLL
HA, HA, HA, HAAH
WHOOOO
GIGGLE

WHAT COULD THEY BE TALKING ABOUT THAT WOULD BE SO DARNED FUNNY?

.... BOYS.

197

April was 10. Elly Patterson looked down at the face of her sleeping daughter. She still had the round cheeks of childhood, but April was a young girl now. Why had the years gone so fast? She hadn't been the easiest kid to live with, but the adventure had been wonderful.

Elly pulled the blanket up and kissed April. "I'll always remember this moment," she thought to herself. "I'm still holding you like a bird in my hand, and, too soon, I'll be letting you go."

The Sunny Days of April
by Andie Parton

Infant child who runs your world
Just a few days old
Tiny fingers tightly curled
It's your heart she holds

Quiet moments in the night
No one else around
Rock her gently, hold her tight
Sing your soothing sounds

Safe inside your loving arms
Stares into your soul
Knows you'll keep her safe from harm
As the years unfold

Little imp who draws on walls
Stamps her feet in rage
Spills her milk and throws her dolls
All the world's her stage

Little princess holding court
Wants to run the world
Bold and sassy, cute and short
Bossy little girl

Sticky fingers, dirty face
Badly need a scrub
Shrieks and giggles, it's a race
To the toy-filled tub

Little darling, precious child
Angel when she sleeps
Daylight comes, she's running wild
Makes a grown man weep

Playing with her in the sand
Castles on the beach
Finding seashells, holding hands
Heaven within reach

Laughing, splashing in the rain
Puddles made to leap
Catching toads and snakes, in vain
Begging you to keep

Watch her growing, see her fly
Reckless, strong, and free
Her tomorrows standing by
Joyful destiny

Independent, kind, and sure
Babe in arms no more
Not just yours to keep secure
The world will watch her soar!